THROUGH THE
VEIL

LISA OHLEN HARRIS

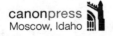

canonpress
Moscow, Idaho

Published by Canon Press
P.O. Box 8729, Moscow, ID 83843
800.488.2034 | www.canonpress.com

Lisa Ohlen Harris, *Through the Veil*
Copyright © 2010 by Lisa Ohlen Harris

Some names have been changed to protect identities.

The following chapters first appeared in the following publications, some in slightly different form: "Immigrant's Granddaughter" as "Through the Looking Glass" in *Eclectica*; "The Pied Piper of Damascus" in *Eclectica*, reprinted in *Rosebud*; "Torn Veil" in *Relief Journal*; "Tell Some Secrets" in *Potomac Review*; "O Barren One" in *Arts & Letters*; "City of Refuge" in *The Summerset Review*; "Evil Eye" in *Jabberwock Review*; "Exiles" in *The Laurel Review*; "Her Face Changes" as "New Year's Day in Amman, Jordan" in *Narrative*; "Wild Olive Shoot" in *The Journal*; and "Flee to the Mountains" in *Under the Sun*.

"Till Moons Shall Wax and Wane No More": Reprinted from *River Teeth*, volume 9, number 1 (fall 2007) by permission of the University of Nebraska Press. © 2008 by the University of Nebraska Press.

Cover painting by Sarah Schoolland.
Cover and interior design by Laura Storm.

Library of Congress Cataloging-in-Publication Data

Harris, Lisa Ohlen.
  Through the veil / Lisa Ohlen Harris.
     p. cm.
  ISBN-13: 978-1-59128-070-5 (pbk.)
  ISBN-10: 1-59128-070-2
  1. Ethnology--Syria--Damascus. 2. Women--Syria--Damascus. 3. Damascus (Syria)--Social life and customs. I. Title.
  GN635.S64H37 2010
  956.9104'2092--dc22
  [B]
                                   2009051953

10 11 12 13 14 15   9 8 7 6 5 4 3 2

Through the Veil

Contents

ACKNOWLEDGMENTS

I want to first of all thank my fellow ethnographic research-ers in Damascus. For leading us well and teaching me what I know about research and surviving cross-culturally, thanks to class leader Steve Unangst. Although I did not make them into "characters" for this book, my research partners Cindy White and Kim Felder will recognize many of the Muslim friends and events in this book. Cindy and Kim, thanks for being by my side so much of the time in Damascus.

I also want to acknowledge my other classmates: the Miller family—Brenda and Eric, Matt and Andy; Eric Chris-tensen and Jeff Porter; and Ann Marie McLeod-Elmore.

And of course the biggest thanks to Todd, who didn't make me fall in love with him until afterwards, who nudged me to write before I sensed the gifting in myself, who has supported me through every sentence and para-graph and chapter.

My extended family, who read my work before pub-lication and granted their blessing even when it included intimate family history—Scott and Michelle Harris, Jeff Harris, Todd and my daughters Laurie, Ashley, Jessica, and Kayla. Also to my mother-in-law Jeanne, who did not live to see this book in print, gratitude and love.

My pastor Dale Smith, ever interested and ever offering faithful praise.

I learned how to write nonfiction by writing *Through the Veil*. Writing and editing thanks must go to my dear friend and fellow essayist, Jill Noel Kandel, as well as Karen Miedrich-Luo and Nancy J. Nordenson—all three of these women are terrific writers and straight-shooting critics. Grateful thanks to Doug Jones, who saw a spark in my early writing even as his eyes rolled back in his head over my purple prose. It's getting better all the time.

CHAPTER 1

DAMASCUS DREAMS

In dreams I walk the winding labyrinth of the Old City. I push through crowds in the bazaar. Daylight filters through cracks and holes in the covered ceiling, like stars piercing the dome of the night sky. Crumbling columns testify that the Roman Empire reached this far. I walk deep into the Old City, and I know where to turn right or left through ancient corridors without numbers or markings. I have no map in my dreams, as I had no map when I walked the streets and lanes of Damascus. I asked my way until I'd memorized the route home by walking it daily, the paths and steps and turnings all soaked into my mind, etched into memory after many tracings.

I speak Arabic in my dreams. When I wake and repeat the words, I laugh at the nonsense that seemed like poetry to my dreaming mind. Other times I am amazed that a dream has resurrected the perfect conjugation of a verb long forgotten. Old friends appear, hands waving as I pass homes, beckoning from open doorways where the smell of a midday meal welcomes. It's all here someplace deep in my memory. Damascus is a part of me.

The streets of ancient Damascus have not changed since I lived there in 1990. They have changed very little over hundreds and thousands of years. The old man who sat on a three-legged stool at the end of our lane—he's gone now. Perhaps his grandson is still there, locking up a shop door and returning to the family home to greet his wife and new son. I would not recognize them. I do not know Damascus as the Damascene. I know it as a foreigner, a wayfarer, one passing through. In deep dreams I remember. When I wake, hours before sunrise, I shake off sleep and I write.

I write the Damascus I love, but sometimes her face blurs and I can't make out details: both dreams and memories are tangled things. They twist themselves around smells and feelings and other memories of times and people far removed. They tumble to the page like a child at play, breathing hard. I calm and comb them, working out the catches and finding the story enmeshed in strands of memory. I write and rewrite, but some memories remain confused and tangled. I work the others, braiding them and tying the ends with reflection and sometimes also tying them with regret.

CHAPTER 2

ALIEN LAND

It woke me from my jet-lagged sleep, it was so loud. I rolled out of bed in the dark and stumbled to the window. Before leaving the U.S. I'd heard a recording of the Call to Prayer. It sounded exotic—distant and haunting. But in real life the Call to Prayer blasted in as if no windows or walls sheltered me. It drove sleep away and made me want to plug my ears. It demanded. I was dragged from my dreams into an alien land on the first morning of my first day in the Middle East.

Under the streetlight outside two men grabbed prayer rugs from the trunk of a taxi and rolled them out, facing away from me. They bowed, knelt, and stood again, touching ears and heart as they made their early morning prayer. The Call to Prayer echoed and faded. The men put their prayer rugs away and lit up cigarettes.

"I could be on Mars," I thought. "And I'm going to live here."

The men finished their cigarettes, got into the taxi, and drove away. The parking lot stretched out large and empty, like the surrounding desert.

On the flight from Amsterdam to Amman I'd slept a dizzy sleep, dreaming of bright mosques in red and orange and green and homes with domed roofs painted in magic-carpet designs. But now in the dim light, everything around me was sand colored and flat roofed—blocks drawn up out of the desert to make a city. The only color was the King Abdullah mosque up on the hill, with its three rotundas of swimming-pool blue.

It was 1990 and I was part of an ethnographic research team. We'd flown into Amman, Jordan, and were spending the night there. In the morning we would take the bus a few hours north, across the Syrian border and up to Damascus, where we would live for three months.

It took weeks before I learned to sleep through the Call to Prayer. Every morning the call went out—and then four more times throughout the day.

Allahu akbar
God is great
There is no God but God
and Mohammed is his prophet
Come and pray
Prayer is better than sleep

CHAPTER 3

THE LOOM

Like a spy I followed them, now pausing to empty an imaginary stone from my shoe, now asking a shop owner the price of a bracelet, all the time watching and waiting for an opportunity.

She wore a billowing Persian *chador:* a length of fabric wrapped around her body, encircling her face. She gripped the chador beneath her chin with one hand as she walked a few steps behind the man I assumed was her husband. Her gaze never drifted beyond his back, as if she were confined by an invisible perimeter that isolated her from the world she moved through. She would have noticed me had she looked. I stood out in Damascus even when I covered my own blond head.

Back home in Oregon I'd been one student of many bundling across campus, heads down in the rain. I didn't stand out in those crowds, and I knew what to expect from the world around me. I recognized the smell of the first cold wind in late fall. I knew the frozen-wet feel of the heavy sky that portended snow.

I'd worked with international students on my campus—Japanese, Arabs, and others. Perhaps those college days foreshadowed the turned-around future, when I would be the foreigner in a strange land. I'd thought myself outgoing when I enrolled in a study tour and came to Damascus. It wasn't so easy, as the foreigner, to be the first to say hello.

I stood so near the woman that I could smell her rose-scented perfume. I heard a cloth merchant in his open stall attempt English and then French with the husband. Because she wore the chador I knew, as the shop owner must have, that this man and this woman were not from Syria. They were Persian, from Iran. They spoke Farsi and not Arabic.

A classmate had noticed that there were more women in chadors near certain mosques in Damascus. One or two focused interviews would give us enough answers to write a brief ethnography on this group for our report. Since I was the outgoing one, I'd been assigned to make contact with one of these women and to bring back answers to the questions jotted in my memo pad. My classmates thought that it would be easy for me. And I suppose it would have been easy, back home. I longed for the Oregon rain to blur the faces around me. In that familiar rain, I would know how to find my destination. With my head down, I would follow the paved walkways across the campus quad.

The man entered a shop and his wife followed. I slipped in as the female clerk greeted them with words I didn't recognize from my Arabic class.

Later that day I would wish I had listened more closely to the greeting in Farsi.

They were interested in a woven rug. They spread it out over the shop's pile of folded weavings. The man stood back to eye the rug while the woman reached out to it, running her fingers across the pattern as if to feel for irregularities. I knew that I should step closer, perhaps feign interest in one of the smaller rugs. But how would I ask

questions of this woman if she spoke no English? Her husband grunted a syllable, and her hand dropped from the
weaving. Then he exited the shop and she followed without
a single glance outside her bubble.

The shopkeeper behind the counter tapped her fingers on
the glass countertop.

"*Privyet*," she said.

I stared at her, trying to fit the word into a variation of
the Arabic greetings I knew.

"Do you, umm, speak English?" I asked.

"Of course. Welcome in Syria." She smiled. "Austra-
lian? G'day, mate."

"I'm from America."

"America? Ah, no wonder you didn't understand."

Through the store window I saw the Iranian couple
take their shoes off at the door to the mosque and disappear inside. I could still go after them. It wasn't too late.

"Did you want to buy a postcard?" she asked me. "I don't
have any with Iranian women on them." She winked.

I felt like a comic character in a black and white movie,
doing a double take. Wasn't winking an American conven-
tion? How did she know?

"My name is Sanaa," she said. "Welcome in Damascus."

This was the hardest part for me. Jumping from
friendly tourist to nosy student researcher. It was one thing
to make friends. Quite another to get down to business
with the ethnographic interview.

"May I ask? That woman—is she Iranian?"

"I have many customers from Iran," Sanaa said. "I
greet them in Farsi. To help them feel at home. Some of the

Iranian families rent homes in my neighborhood. I know them very well."

It was easier than I'd thought.

"My customers come from every country, and I greet each of them in their own language." Sanaa pulled two chairs together behind the counter. "Come, rest here with me."

I hesitated, not sure whether I was avoiding my research goals or meeting them. But I wanted to sit with Sanaa. She reminded me of my days working with international students. Just as Sanaa had learned to greet her customers in their own language, I had a goal for myself—in that other life, back in Oregon—to learn a phrase or two in the language of each of my students.

I drew my mind back to the day's research topic.

"You say some of your neighbors are from Iran? Why do they live in Damascus?"

She took a thermos and small handleless cup from under the counter.

"Real Arabic coffee. From the Bedouin. It's the best."

Sanaa poured a splash of dark coffee into a traditional Arabic coffee cup—more a small bowl than a cup. The bitter coffee tasted unpleasant, but I drank.

"A small sip is enough," she said. "Then rock the cup like this, and you have thanked your host." I waggled the cup; she took it from me, sipping and waggling for herself before setting the cup down behind the counter.

"There," she said. "That's the Bedouin way to make friends."

Her lightly accented English was grammatically perfect. Why didn't she answer my questions? Again I asked her about the Iranians living in Damascus. I piled up the questions: how many and why and whether they stayed for months or years.

Sanaa reached for a stack of photos tucked under the cash box behind the counter.

"These are the Bedouin women who make our rugs," she told me. What was the connection between these photos and my question? Perhaps another day I'd be assigned to research the Bedouin, and I would wish for an opportunity like this. Sanaa held the stack of photos out, and I took them from her.

The first photo showed two women sitting cross-legged around a tray, drinking from handleless cups. In another photo, one of the women held a calculator.

The next was a close-up of the loom under wrinkled hands. Blue and rusty orange yarn stretched lengthwise for maybe two yards, waiting for the cross-threads that would set a design in the work and make it a rug instead of a length of wool threads. When Sanaa gestured to the finished rugs at the back of the store, I thought of the Iranian woman. What would I have done if she had turned around, looked straight into my eyes, and spoken to me in a language I didn't understand?

Later that day I stood waiting at the bus station. Beside me a thin man smoked with quick puffs, tapping ashes onto the ground. Soon the bus would arrive and the crowd around us would start pushing. I moved, positioning myself away from the burning cigarette.

As the bus pulled in I felt hands on my upper back, but already the crowd compressed so I couldn't turn around and see who touched me. The hands stayed my back, propelling me through the crowd. I fell to my knees on the bus stairs, and the hands lifted me to my feet, still pressing me forward, over the threshold and onto the bus. I stepped over a glowing cigarette butt in the aisle and looked for an empty spot.

I sat next to a woman who was turned to look out the window, a length of floral fabric flowing over the back of her head. Her bright chador was different from any I'd seen in Damascus.

The bus rolled out of the lot, lurching until we were on the main road. My seatmate swayed then steadied, still looking out the window, her back to me. The pattern on her chador was woven, not printed. At her shoulders, black threads seemed to break free of the design and poke right through the weave. The threads were her hair. They blended with the pattern in the fabric, except that the hairs poking through looked stiff compared to the soft drape of the chador as its fabric flowed down the back of her head, over her shoulders, to the seat.

She turned to me and I became part of her enclosed world. Her eyes wrinkled around the sides, and she lowered the fabric to reveal a smile. Around her face wisps of black hair slipped out from the chador, thick like her eyelashes. She spoke in Farsi—too quickly for me to parrot the words. I responded in Arabic. She smiled, shook her head and touched my hand, speaking again in Farsi. I answered in English this time. Again she shook her head and spoke, very quietly, with tentative, choppy words.

"*Konichi-wa.*"

The words hung for a moment, vaguely familiar. Then somewhere out of the Iranian woman's past and mine, an old thread emerged and twisted into the weave.

"Konichi-wa," I said.

Words I'd memorized to welcome my Japanese students now connected me with this woman from Iran. In Japanese, she asked me how I was and learned that I was fine. Already running out of phrases, I mentioned several menu items from my favorite Japanese restaurant back home. She countered by naming the islands of Japan. Then she smiled and tucked loose threads into the hem of her chador, while I wondered why she had Japanese words to offer.

In Bedouin carpets like the ones Sanaa showed me, there are no loose threads. Even while the carpet is being formed in long strands of wool on the loom, each thread is connected, stretching out as a single, not yet complete, piece of work. Looking out the bus window, over the floral shoulder of the Iranian woman, I imagined a long woven carpet unrolling just ahead of me, through Old City corridors and down busy Damascus streets.

She got off the bus before I did and joined two black-robed women who exited from the rear door and met her on the curb. By the time the bus came to my stop, near the end of the route, there were few passengers left. I climbed the steps from the street into the Old City, just a few lanes away from home.

Along one narrow corridor, a woman swept dust and pebbles out of her front door so they scattered to the corners of the lane. I looked past her into the open courtyard of her home. All along the edge of the inner balcony hung carpets, blue and orange and gold, airing in the sun while she cleaned her floors. They were in the same colors as the Bedouin rugs in Sanaa's shop, the same colors as the rugs in the snapshots. Was there connection here, too? I imagined an invisible thread, like the long warp on a loom, connecting past to future and woman to woman. She stopped sweeping and smiled, gesturing an invitation for me to come into her home. Perhaps there would be no common threads at all, just an awkward cup of tea and a wasted hour. But I wouldn't know unless I tested the strength of the line.

"Welcome," she said. "Welcome in Syria."

I stepped through the door and into the inner courtyard.

CHAPTER 4

THE PIED PIPER
OF DAMASCUS

"You will come to our home."

She spoke to me in Arabic, in the imperative. Her hand gripped my arm. I felt like a third grader trapped by a gang of bullies in a deserted schoolyard—no one could see my distress, surrounded by this tent of veiled women all wearing long black robes. I pulled my arm down and away; she held on and jerked back. The women stood in a tight circle around me, touching my arms, my shoulders, reaching under my sleeves to feel my fair skin. When my scarf fell back, exposing my blond hair, I heard one of them say the Arabic word for *gold*.

Along with my American classmates I lived with an Arab family in the Old City. I'd been on my way home from the university this day, pushing through the usual crowds in the big covered bazaar, Hamadiyye Souk. There was something slick on the ground, some bit of gunk there in the souk, and I slipped on it, skidding then catching myself. I looked down expecting to see a smear of over-ripe fruit under my foot. It was a crushed mouse, its fur glossy with blood. I scraped the sole of my shoe against the ground. Disgusting. It didn't seem possible that I'd killed the thing—surely it had been run over by one of the horse-drawn carts that rumbled through the covered market daily. Oh, ick. I still felt the lump of gore, though I scuffed my foot on the ground with every other step. I hadn't believed my Kurdish friend when she told me that the Old City was full of mice, and rats, too. Now I'd seen for myself.

Hamadiyye Souk empties onto an open-air breezeway with Roman columns. Ruins of an ancient temple to the Roman god Jupiter line the walkway from the end of the souk to the big mosque at the edge of the Old City. I passed the temple and started to cut around the mosque wall, over on the southern side where the gold merchants have their shops all in a row. I stopped to lift my foot and see if my shoe was still mucked up with mouse. Nope. Dusty, but no mouse remnants. In the shop window before me, dozens upon dozens of 18- and 22-carat bangle bracelets, necklaces, and rings hung in tiers along the window-length display rod. Each shop boasted a similar display of jewelry, hung to form glimmering curtains in gold so pure it was nearly orange.

Back at our Old City home I was trying to read through a chapter or two in the book of Exodus each morning. I would rise soon after the first Call to Prayer and in the early light I would open my Bible and read about the building of God's tabernacle. It seemed that God was greedy for gold. In the Holy of Holies, everything that God might touch had to be pure, heavy, magnificent gold. The average Hebrew never saw the glorious golden room in the tabernacle, because God ordered curtains of goats' hair to be made as an outer tent over the whole thing.

The Bedouin live in goats' hair tents even today. They weave the coarse, dark hair with loose stitches, allowing for ventilation on the many hot days. When it's rainy the threads swell and tighten, making the tent waterproof. But Bedouin aren't poor—not all of them. These days it's common to see a satellite dish nestled in the truck bed outside a goats' hair tent, generator humming in the background. Bedouin women wear necklaces and bangles of gold under their robes, adorned like every Middle Eastern bride. A woman's gold is her insurance policy. If her husband divorces her or she's left widowed and hungry she can sell her gold, ring by ring, to feed herself and her children. It's a convenient form of savings. It's always within reach. Women in Damascus safely walk through alleys and poor neighborhoods wearing hundreds of dollars worth of jewelry jingling on wrists and flashing on fingers

The group of women stood in front of a shop window where gold necklaces crowded so tightly on a display hook that they looked like a rope. The women wore dark robes embroidered across the bodice—I could tell that they weren't from Damascus. Five women, but only two men. All of them wearing wedding rings.

In Syria, it's unusual for a man to take multiple wives, even though Islam and the Syrian government allow it. An extra wife would be too great an economic hardship for most, because Islam requires fair and equal treatment for each wife. Five women and two men. If these robed women were multiple wives as I suspected, then under their sleeves each carried exactly the same amount of gold jewelry, gram for gram, as her fellow wife.

The women stared at my fair features, distracted from the rows of bracelets and necklaces and rings by a better prize. The men stood apart from their wives, as if watching a show. I brushed against one of the women as I passed and pardoned myself in Arabic before moving to go around her. She looked directly at me and stepped back, opening the circle to draw me in. The women's black robes closed around me.

One of them leaned closer. Bracelets jangled under her sleeves, making music as she gestured. This was before she grabbed me, but already she stood so close that I could smell garlic on her breath. Her sister-wife stood beside her; one of the sister's front teeth was capped in gold.

And both of them had *blue eyes*.

My Arab friends in Damascus were dark-skinned, dark-haired, dark-eyed. Arab coloring is a study in desert shadows: olive skin and browns and tans. I occasionally saw Arabs with green or blue eyes, and it always surprised me. My own blue eyes come from a family tree rooted in northern climes of Sweden, Germany, and France. They're a recessive trait, European. But these women—nomads, probably—were part of the ancient Middle Eastern desert where the sun bakes everything brown; why did they have blue eyes like mine? Though I was trying to remember phrases from my conversational Arabic class, I kept thinking of the word *swarthy* as they jostled and grabbed at me. I thought of pirates and of slave traders.

Her Arabic was broad, hard for me to understand. I had minimal conversational skills in one dialect of a language that spans dozens of countries and cultures over two continents. Classical written Arabic is unified, one like Allah, but dialect differences in spoken Arabic make mutual intelligibility tricky, sometimes impossible for even the native speaker. The effort of listening made me feel as if I were underwater, holding my breath in order to keep my focus. My head whirled from the closeness of black fabric and the heat of their bodies around me. After each question I guessed at the meaning and answered *yes* or *no* in Arabic; the woman cooed and laughed. She embraced me and then she kept a hand on me, gripping my upper arm. Now I understood every Arabic word.

"You will come to our home."

I could almost see the Bedouin camp where they would keep me hostage, isolated in the desert, far away from embassies and other foreigners to uncover my plight. Why did she want me, anyway? Did she see something in my eyes, something of her own blue-eyed ancestry, connecting us back through time and culture?

It may be myth set in the heart of history. The records are questionable, but accounts of the Crusades speak of children's movements in 1212, between the Fourth and Fifth Crusades. In France thousands of young children left their carts and flocks and whatever else they were doing and ran one after the other, swarming the hills, leaving homes and lands, journeying to Jerusalem. The children rushed in droves, following after a twelve-year-old peasant boy, Stephen, who called them all to come. History doesn't record much about Stephen, except that he was a skinny orphan with bushy brown hair and bright blue eyes. Christ came to him in a vision and told him to gather the little children and go to Jerusalem. And the children—girls along with the boys—crowded after Stephen, following him south toward the sea and the Holy Land.

Meanwhile in Germany a second children's crusade formed under the spell of another pre-teen magic boy, Nicholas. The old Pied Piper story comes out of these bits of history, so whatever trick it was that Stephen had up his sleeve, there was something of mystery or myth about him right from the start.

The children marched south toward the sea, expecting that when they arrived at the Mediterranean, the waters would part for them. When the waves kept rolling and no dry land appeared, kind shipholders gave the children free passage, cramming ships full from bottom to top with these naive—by now also ragged and hungry—European ambassadors. The children who survived the ride were sold into slavery in Egypt and the Levant, ironically living out their lives subject to those they thought would bow down at their own little feet when they entered Palestine. Their blue eyes still look out from Middle Eastern crowds through the souls of their Arab descendents.

In my own bed in our Old City home that night, I saw what might have been. I was the fourth wife, making the best of my misfortune. I would be the type to submit, not to plan an escape. Does that make me a victim and not a conqueror? What if my own courageous ancestors had taken off over the hills with Stephen, pioneering to North Africa and beyond before they even hit puberty? They wouldn't be my ancestors if they had been sold into slavery in the Middle East and married and had children and grandchildren until nothing was left of the European ancestry except an occasional blue-eyed child. My own forefathers resisted; we were left behind when adventure beckoned with blue eyes.

Meanwhile, the blood of my ancestral cousins—the ones who heard Stephen's call and followed—mixed with their dark-skinned captors, perhaps buying freedom for themselves and for their descendents. Those blue-eyed sisters may have been my distant cousins, and I resisted the family reunion. I liked to think of myself as an adventurer, but surprising turns of plan held little delight for me. Rather than jump into opportunity, I would stand firm or turn and make my way home.

I would have been the child left behind when the Pied Piper came to town.

In my dreams I heard the chinking of gold bracelets hidden under her heavy robe as she beckoned me. It might have been the glint of the gold tooth in the desert sunshine that knocked me out of my momentary trance in the company of those veiled women. I ducked and tugged away from the blue-eyed woman; she held my scarf, and I let it slide off in her hand. It was a blue scarf with metallic threads running through it. I'd searched a long time through a stack of scarves in the souk to find the exact blue to match my eyes.

I hurried around the mosque, past the old men smoking water pipes at the tea shop just down from the gold souk. I looked back before I rounded the corner—to check and be sure that one of the women wasn't coming after me.

They were gone. As if they'd been swallowed up by one of the stone walls. I don't think they could have all crowded into one of the gold shops—they wouldn't have fit. But somehow, when I ran away, they all disappeared.

The Damascus crowds pushed past me. My ankle and foot were sore. I must have sprained something when I slipped in the souk, or maybe when I pulled away from the woman. My foot felt tender and my shoe too tight.

As I limped home, I thought about the adventure I might be missing. Now the blue-eyed women were going back to their village or camp, riding in the truck bed and feeling the desert wind tug at their head coverings. Now they told tales of the pale foreigner with the golden hair who refused to come. They laughed and sang, their blue eyes flashing. I imagined that one of the women tied my blue scarf about her wrist and reached her arm up high into the wind. My scarf stretched and flapped like a banner above the black robed women as they streamed across the desert, and the gold threads sparkled in the sun.

CHAPTER 5

IMMIGRANT'S
GRANDDAUGHTER

Traditional Middle Eastern homes climb a hilly Kurdish neighborhood to the north of the ancient walled city of Damascus. The poorest Kurds climb to the topmost lanes, to homes without electricity or running water. This is my first day of ethnographic research among the Kurds. I'm in the right part of Damascus—now it's a matter of finding someone who will speak with me. I enter a small shop and ask the young woman at the cashbox if she speaks English.

"Little," she says, tugging her scarf forward. When I ask her if she lives in this area she shakes her head to show she does not understand. I look around for a few minutes and purchase a hair clip before leaving the shop. As I leave she's right behind me, pulling down the metal door that lowers over the shop's entrance and front windows.

"English," she says, smiling and gesturing for me to follow her up one steep lane and then another. This is the amazing thing about Damascus. People love to help the foreigner. Because of this I find it's easy to fill my notebook with ethnographic interviews. It seems that anyone I ask has a sister, a cousin, a neighbor who speaks English, and they're willing to drop whatever they're doing to help. As

I follow this young woman I watch for landmarks and try to remember each turn so that I can find my way out of this hilly Damascus neighborhood where all the front doors look alike.

The young veiled woman smiles back at me as she leads me up and up the dirt lanes. She places her hand on a doorknob and pushes it open, calling out in Arabic. Immediately we are welcomed with kisses by another young woman who pulls me past the courtyard fountain and into the dim parlor that opens off of the courtyard. "I studied English in school," she says in a rush. "Welcome in our home. Welcome in Syria."

Her name is Huda, and she is the granddaughter of a Kurdish immigrant.

My first day of kindergarten, I sat next to a thin girl with glasses.

"My name is S-U-S-A-N," she said. "Will you be my best friend?"

It was that easy. Susan lived a block away. She had tiny turtles the size of the buttons on my mother's nubby wool coat. After we'd played out a long afternoon Susan would walk me home and I would walk her back. We were together nearly every day after school and on weekends—until my mother found out that Susan would play at my house only if I gave her a toy each time she visited.

My friendship with Susan faded as I grew weary of playing only the games she chose and the roles she gave me. I learned early to steer clear of the bossy girls. Yet I remember Susan with fondness: my first friend. And from her I learned the secret password to friendship. A world of potential friends stretched out before me. At school, in parks and playgrounds, in ballet class and at the library, I made my selections carefully, then spoke companionship into being.

"Will you be my friend?"

Huda is twenty years old, but she wears the same long robe, embellished at the yoke with embroidery, that older Syrian women wear. It's a relaxed choice in clothing to reflect the comfortable lifestyle of a woman who works at home and rarely goes out in public. She has little need for dress shoes or tucked-in blouses or headscarves. Whenever I visit Huda, she takes up her work—needle and thread. My work is research so I sit with pencil and notepad, asking Huda about family networks and religious devotion among her family and neighbors. Huda works from home sewing piecework for a local women's tailor. She answers my questions as she stitches. So far I've learned from Huda that her grandfather was a Kurdish immigrant who came to Damascus from Turkey more than fifty years ago. His children, including Huda's father, spoke Arabic at school and at home. The Kurdish language was lost to her family in a generation.

On my list of questions for today is *Kurdish women's roles in the home and workplace.* I ask Huda how long she has done this work and why it is she works from home while her sister works down the street at the shop where I first met her. Huda holds the fabric lightly, stitching as she tells me the story.

When she was about ten her father surprised her with the wonderful news that he'd arranged with the tailor for

Huda to do some simple sewing. She was to work at home, and she would be paid. He trusted she would use small stitches and sew four collars a week.

Two of the girls a grade older than Huda were also sewing for the tailor. They stopped by his shop before school one day a week to deliver their finished work in exchange for wages, while their classmates watched with envy. It was a good job for a girl—the sort of skill a young man would be pleased to find in a potential wife. Huda's sharp eyes and small fingers would be trained to work the stitches that made this tailor sought after. A perfect job, her father told her, because she could do it at home and never have to worry about sitting next to a man in the workplace. Once she started the sewing, her studies did not seem very important to Huda, though her father insisted that they were, that the right young man would want a woman who could both read and sew.

Huda's father died before she finished high school.

My grandfather was a tailor. He came to America in 1928 on the Swedish ship *Gripsholm*. He was eighteen, and he came alone. In Seattle he built the American dream, first working long hours and long years for an established tailor, and later opening his own business. He met and married my grandmother, who was the daughter of another Swedish immigrant.

"I'll take you back to the Old Country one day," he used to promise me. "The hills are so green in spring your heart will ache." He painted a Sweden so real in my imagination that it became my Old Country, too.

"I'm Swedish," I used to say to my playmates.

"You're American," my mother corrected me.

There were gifts brought back from Sweden through the years. The wooden clogs my brother and I called "clap shoes" because of their delightful noise on hard floors. The ivory colored sweater I wore through high school, embellished with flowers made of twists and knots of orange and red and blue wool. All these things were outgrown, passed down, worn out.

I still keep a small book from Grandpa, the one gift not selected by my grandmother. It's a palm-sized travel guide, titled, *Say It in Swedish!* To the first page he taped one of his business cards, upside-down so he could write on the back of it: *I love you Lisa—Grandpa Emil.* The card is taped near the top, so I can still flip it up to read the front. Emil, Custom Tailor. An image adorns the card—a simple silhouette of an Old World tailor sitting cross-legged on his sewing table as his stitches fly.

By the time she was twelve, Huda's stitches were so lovely that the tailor assigned embroidery work rather than simple sewing. Her last year of school, English was the only subject that captured Huda. She loved that the manuscript writing was all backward and stick-like, so different from the flowing script of Arabic or the smooth movement of needle and thread. She took pride in stitching her English sentences together, each detail of the syntax exactly in its place.

Huda ushers me into the enclosed world of a conservative Muslim woman at home. I'm in and out of taxis and buses. I already know a lot about public life in Damascus. I walk through the bazaars and the university campus. When men call to me, whether in Arabic or in English, I look straight ahead and pretend I don't understand their words. The few times I am pinched or stroked in public by a strange man I make angry eye contact. I rebuke him loudly, to make public his sin in this culture of shame. Old women will come to my defense, rebuking any man who treats a woman with such disrespect. Once again I know a secret password. I feel powerful and strong. There are things I like about being a woman in this culture.

Huda knows that my study group lives with an Arab family in the Old City. What she doesn't know is that some of my classmates—my housemates—are young men. In nearly every way Huda is my opposite. She has no brothers and the only man who ever sees her unveiled is her mother's brother, her guardian. The house she and her sisters and mother live in is owned by this uncle.

One day I meet Uncle, when he comes to check on the family. He speaks a few phrases of English, as do so many Syrians, because they're required to take either French or English classes in the government schools. I try out some Arabic phrases I'm learning. He seems kind. His heart must be huge to take on the financial support of his sister and her three daughters. Uncle is a strong wall, guarding Huda from the dangers of the world outside the courtyard door. Because I'm growing to love Huda, I feel respect and even affection for Uncle.

What does Huda learn from me? Perhaps through my eyes she catches a glimpse of her own world, widened slightly. When I tell her about the view from my rooftop in the Old City of Damascus, she shrugs.

"It's dirty in the Old City," she says. "And rats every place. Uncle shops for us in Hamadiyye Souk, but I have never been there."

"You've never been to Old Damascus?" The taxi ride across town takes no more than ten minutes.

"Why would I? In my house I am happy."

A pea-soup fog. That's what Dad called it. As Dad and Grandpa unloaded boxes I snuck up to the attic of our new home in Oregon. Through blurry leaded glass the acreage beyond our circular driveway was lost in the fog. We could be a house afloat in space, like something in a science fiction movie. Alone.

This was the night of my sixteenth birthday. A California girl transplanted from sundresses into flannel shirts and jeans. *Sweet sixteen and never been kissed.* Grandma baked a cake. My California friends were far behind, back where I grew up, back where the fog lifted by midmorning and the sun shone warm. There was a boy back there . . . but he had never kissed me, and now he never would.

Grandma brought out the cake. How pitiful. This should be a blowout of a party. I should have had my first date by now. Grandpa leaned over and put his arm around my shoulder.

"Don't be so down. There are boyfriends out there for you." He kissed me on the cheek.

It was no comfort to me in my self-pity, but I sensed that the kiss was a deep gesture. Grandpa knew why I was so grumpy. He had not been much older than sixteen when he set off to America alone. He, too, left friends behind.

I always wanted to be an adventurer like Grandpa. As a little girl visiting the house my dad grew up in, the house Grandpa built, I explored the "woods" out back. As I grew older, the woods seemed to shrink until I saw with the eyes of an adult that it was only a wide jumble of trees and undergrowth along the property line. But for a small child, exploring, that swath of woods became the world.

One day I knock on Huda's door and she answers breathless and laughing. She wears a modest coat over her dress, with stockings and heels instead of her usual house slippers. I hardly recognize Huda with her head covered by a scarf, tightly pinned so it won't slip. Instead of welcoming me into the house, Huda heaves the front door closed behind her and links her arm in mine. We walk five minutes around the corner and up the hill to a neighbor's home, that of Huda's older cousin. The large, inner courtyard is full of folding chairs, arranged in a huge circle. There must be over fifty women here. I've heard that large gatherings in homes are illegal in Syria—to prevent political conclaves, I suspect—but there is nothing clandestine to this open-air meeting.

"My family," Huda whispers to me as we remove our scarves and take our places in the circle of women. Over five hundred members of her extended family live within walking distance, Huda says. I must misunderstand her— five hundred relatives in this very neighborhood? Huda insists. She licks her finger, bends down and writes *500* on the dusty tile of the garden courtyard.

Huda's sister is here. She ties a filmy scarf low around her hips while the aunts and cousins keep chatting. Someone brings out a tape recorder and snaps in a cassette. Music rises and swirls. The dancer's hips flow and thrust in such intimate movements I have to look away.

"You dance now, Lisa," Huda says. "American style."

A tray of small glasses is offered and I take one carefully, holding it by the rim to avoid burning myself. I don't want to dance in front of these women. I protest and avoid meeting Huda's eyes by ducking to drink the too-sweet tea, so sugared that it feels thick like syrup on my tongue.

"Dance for us," Huda laughs as she pushes me to my feet.

Her sister ties the scarf low on my hips and someone turns up the music.

Huda must have been learning to read and write in Arabic the year I took ballet, when I was six or seven. Memories of my weekly ballet classes distort like a fever dream. I was Gulliver in Lilliput, my clumsy feet like sloshing boats in the midst of a sea of tiny slippered toes skimming lightly from first position to second.

Was the dance floor warped? The studio built on a hill? The wooden floor seemed to slope in my direction, because the teacher constantly slipped down to my end of the class to straighten all the parts of me that stuck out: chunky knees, belly, and bottom.

During the final program at the end of the session, I lost my place in the dance line and jigged in the wrong direction on the wrong foot for the remainder of the number. Dance wasn't my gift, they said.

These Kurdish women don't know what American dancing should look like. I tap my foot and a light cheer rises from one side of the room. I twirl. For all they know I could be a trained dancer from America on tour in Syria. I jump from one foot to the other, doing The Pony, my loose hair flapping as I bounce. The older women stop chatting to watch. They smile at me and begin to clap in time with my jumping. One grandmother hollers out a "lalalalala" at the high pitch right where her voice cracks. Just when I am inspired to try even fancier moves another single woman pushes me back to my seat, laughing, and takes my place.

Huda raises an eyebrow at me, grins, and holds out her teacup in a mock salute. I love it here. I don't belong, yet they all move aside to make room for me, just as I am. I find my own scarf and wipe my sweaty forehead, then spread the damp fabric across the back of my chair to dry.

The chatting breaks off. The dancer freezes. Every third woman grabs for her scarf. Someone clicks off the tape player. At the courtyard door stands Huda's uncle. The mass of women sort themselves out into those related to him by blood, with heads uncovered, and those related by marriage, scrambling to hide their hair under scarves. Uncle stares at something on the ground by his shoe until the rush for scarves settles, and then he steps through the courtyard and into the parlor, where I can just see him in the shadows. The hostess leaves the circle to pour tea for Uncle. He stays only a few minutes.

Heads remain covered even after Uncle leaves. Though the women chat and laugh, there is no more music. No one dances.

Grandpa danced with me. I rode on his big shoes, so it didn't matter whether I knew the steps for myself. When Auntie quickened the pace on her accordion to squeeze-pull-squeeze out a merry Swedish polka, Grandpa danced so fast my pigtails swished against my ears. He stopped when Grandma came into the room. He extended an arm to her and I stepped off his feet and sat next to Auntie on the piano stool. My grandparents flew around the coffee table and sofa in three-quarter time.

The next time I visit Huda, her sister answers the door and opens it wide. I step into the courtyard and catch sight of Huda's robe disappearing into the bedroom area of the house. In a moment she comes out to greet me. She wears her usual house robe, but a scarf covers her head in *hijab*.

The term hijab, commonly used by Syrians as a synonym for scarf or veil, is actually the Arabic word for "curtain," or "covering." Hijab can refer to any clothing worn for modesty's sake—especially in the presence of unrelated men.

"Are we going out again today, Huda?" I wouldn't mind another opportunity to dance.

"Come, sit, drink tea," she says.

We visit outside by the fountain instead of in the parlor. Huda holds some embroidery in her lap, but she doesn't take up the needle. She shifts in her seat and looks toward the courtyard door.

"My uncle told me to wear the hijab for you."

"I don't understand. Why wear it at home?"

"Uncle tells me—how can I say it . . ." she won't look at me. "He tells us that an infidel should not see us uncovered. He says that you are as a man to us."

How does Uncle know that I am not a Muslim? I always cover my head as soon as I come into Huda's conservative neighborhood. I often cover my head anyway, to keep from getting pinched. I'm not a man; what kind of reasoning did Uncle use to make up this nonsense? And I somehow know that my honor is the issue here. Huda's uncle must think I'm not a virgin. He must fear that my wild influence will pull Huda outside the purity of Islam. Huda believes what her uncle tells her.

I see myself through Huda's eyes—through Uncle's eyes: the free, unmarried woman who travels alone, living in Damascus while the men in my family carry on their own business back in North America and offer me no protection at all from the rest of the world. I want to protest that I *am* a virgin . . . but what pure Muslim woman would believe me? Does a virgin share a home—a bathroom, even—with a bunch of single men? Does a righteous woman walk through the city alone with her head uncovered, her arms bare?

A few months after I return to the U.S. an envelope arrives with exotic Damascus stamps. I open it carefully, slitting the top smoothly rather than tearing open the flap. Written on a piece of lined paper that looks as if it were torn from a college exam booklet, the note's pink-ruled margin is on the right side, rather than the left. She writes in English, only this:

> Dear Lisa,
> When you left there became a hole in my heart.
> Huda

CHAPTER 6

TILL MOONS SHALL WAX AND WANE NO MORE

"Where is it?" Maisa asked, chewing the end of her pencil. "Where is the rose?"

We sat on the cold steps outside a mosque near Damascus University. Maisa held her pencil above an exam booklet with President Assad's picture printed on the cover. I had a slim volume of Faulkner, in English, open to a story I vaguely remembered from my own college lit class: "A Rose for Emily." An old maid and a house that was a tomb. Arsenic, a dead man, and a bed for a bier. Was there a rose? I couldn't remember.

"What is the meaning?" Maisa rubbed her eraser on the page until the sentences blurred to a dark cloud.

Before we had a chance to discuss the story, an old man came out from the mosque and scolded us because my head was uncovered and my sleeves didn't reach far enough past my elbows. Maisa didn't make eye contact with the *imam*, but she picked up her book and pencil and led me away from the building. Whether Muslim or Christian, a woman's head must be covered to enter a mosque— I knew that—but the disgruntled imam made it clear that a foreigner should be covered at all times, at least near a holy place.

"It's my fault," Maisa said. "This is happening because of my dream."

Maisa had invited me to sit in on her American literature class earlier that day. It seems that O'Connor and Faulkner speak to the world's university students as much as any foreign policy. Through them students in Syria get a freaky glimpse of life in the West.

As the students settled in the lecture hall, Maisa whispered to me that she was not sleeping well. When she prayed, she felt that Allah wasn't listening to her. Earlier that week Maisa dreamed that she'd lost her virginity. A good dream is from Allah, she told me, and some dreams emerge from the events of the day and mean nothing. But a bad dream, such a dishonorable, wicked dream as this can only come from Satan. The dream defiled her, and she'd been working off the impurity by increasing her prayers from five a day to eight. Then another dream came from Satan—this time a filthy dog leaping to Maisa's chest and pushing her down, pinning her to the ground, contaminating her by its unclean parts, by its saliva and feces. The spectral dog canceled out the prayers she'd made as restitution for the earlier dream about losing her virginity. Satan was coming for her, Maisa said. She only hoped he wouldn't come again.

"But it was a dream," I said. "You didn't do anything wrong."

Maisa looked at me, the skin between her eyebrows pressed together in confusion. "Yes, I did. I had the dreams."

She would have to pray faithfully for days—weeks even—before God would hear her. And Ramadan was coming soon. Perhaps she would fast ahead of time, to get ready, she told me. As long as there were no more dreams . . .

Maisa lived with her widowed mother in a village outside of Damascus. She invited me to come home with her from the university, to break the fast at sunset and spend the night there in the village.

We stood in stocking feet at the door of the apartment, our shoes lined up neatly with the other empty pairs outside the entry. Maisa pulled off her scarf even before we were through the front door; she dropped it along with her books on a chair as she hurried to the kitchen where her mother was finishing preparations for the daily sunset feast.

Maisa wouldn't let me help her set plates on the table, so I went to put my overnight bag in her bedroom. Twin beds stood across the room, flanking the window. After setting my bag down on one of the beds, I looked outside. Seven mosques pierced the sky above the flat roofs of the village. Just ten minutes earlier we'd come off the bus into crowds of people rushing to get home to break the fast. Now the village was a ghost town, sand and dust blowing through the empty streets like some *Twilight Zone* episode. Maisa came to the bedroom door and said, "It's almost time."

In the dining room Maisa's mother rushed the last hot dishes from the kitchen. The sun was setting, and when it dipped below the horizon the Call to Prayer would signal it was time to break the day's fast.

Steam rose from chicken cooked in yogurt. The fragrance taunted us. We were hungry, but it was not yet time to eat. Maisa turned on the television to watch for the sunset Call to Prayer. File footage of pigeons flying through the courtyard of a deserted mosque filled the screen; then the Call to Prayer sang out from the television several seconds before the same sound rose from mosques around the village. We ate.

Maisa and her mother refused my help clearing the table, but while they washed dishes in the kitchen I managed to grab a sponge to wipe down the plastic tablecloth. When I came to rinse the sponge, Maisa looked embarrassed. She lifted it from my hand. "Take your rest," she said. "Sit down and read."

So she vanquished me from the kitchen. That's the phrase Faulkner used. "So she vanquished them, horse and foot, just as she had vanquished their fathers thirty years before about the smell."[†] What a creepy story. Sitting down with the book again, I skimmed to the part when Miss Emily finally dies an old maid. One upstairs bedroom is sealed like a tomb. There the townspeople find Emily's lover in her marriage bed, his clothing and flesh decayed for so many years they crumble to dust on his skeleton. She'd slipped him the arsenic so he'd never leave her, and he never did. I thought I remembered that the rose would be there on the pillow beside the corpse, but no—on the pillow is a long gray hair of Miss Emily.

Hadn't I read somewhere that lovers in the Old South would give each other a flower, usually a rose, for a keepsake? A young belle might press the flower to dry and preserve it, to hold it close to her heart when her lover was away. I did it myself when I was a teen, with that first rose from that first boy. On the day he gave me the rose, I

[†]William Faulkner, "A Rose for Emily," *Collected Stories of William Faulkner* (New York: Vintage Books, 1995), 121.

hung it upside-down to dry. I snuck a clothespin out of the laundry basket and clipped the rose's stem to my winter coat—deep in my closet so my brothers wouldn't tease me about saving it. Mom always said that you have to decide right away with roses. Either you enjoy them for a few days, maybe a week in the vase, or else you hang them upside-down to dry, so you can have them forever. With roses you've got to kill them to keep them.

Maisa read the entire story three times, she'd told me— the closing passage so many times she couldn't keep count. It was disturbing, unnatural, but there had to be meaning in it, some redeeming crystal. The last page of the story was torn about one-third of the way down, as if Maisa had turned the page too hard and fast in her zeal to find the meaning. All that was missing was a little fingertip-shaped crescent—not enough gone to obscure the words.

Well, the story creeped me out, too. Even more when I thought of it through Maisa's eyes. The Prophet Mohammed urged Muslims to bury their dead within twenty-four hours—Islam doesn't permit embalming. When Maisa selected a Christian story from the West, she read and reread how Miss Emily kept a cadaver until it stank . . . worse, until it stopped stinking.

When a Muslim dies the body must be prepared for burial through a ritual cleansing. Each body part is cleaned in a prescribed way, and then the corpse is wrapped in one or two white sheets for burial. Muslims are always buried with their heads facing the same direction. In death, as in prayer, they aim toward Mecca.

I closed Faulkner. How odd that this was how Maisa learned about the Christian West. A southern old maid poisons her beau and keeps his dead body in a bridal chamber so she can play pretend. Her neighbors play pretend, too, because when the body starts to decay and stink they wait until night to sneak over to Miss Emily's and sprinkle lime around her house. What if I'd been one of the townspeople? I like to think I would have drawn close to Miss Emily a long time before she poisoned her suitor. I like to imagine myself bringing Faulkner's story to life: walking into the sepulcher and leading Miss Emily out into the day.

I imagine Miss Emily whispering her nightmares to me, unveiling her fears of desertion and failure. I see myself throwing open her curtains so sunlight would transform her world from darkness to light.

But it's hard to see clearly in a dank and dusty place. It's hard to think straight when you can smell death. Perhaps I would have joined the townspeople, all of us sprinkling lime in the dark and creeping home through the shadows to sleep on our own clean sheets.

Maisa and I went to bed fairly early that night, not long after she made the evening prayer. Between our beds the Ramadan half-moon was bright, perfectly framed by the window. It was a cool night at the end of a warm day, the window open slightly. The fresh outside air smelled of jasmine flowers, and I was glad to sleep.

A splintering crash woke me. I heaved the blanket over my head and rolled toward the wall to protect myself from flying glass. I heard the boom-ba-boom-boom of explosions, like cymbals and drums outside the building. We had to get to a lower level. I looked toward Maisa, my neck, my hands pulsing with the rhythm of the bombardment. My friend sat up, very slowly—didn't she sense the danger? She put her legs over the side of the bed. Maisa was too calm, feeling around with her feet until she found her shower-shoe slippers. It had gotten cold overnight, and she pulled the window shut.

It wasn't broken.

"I will pray, and then it is breakfast," she said to me. It was still dark. She slipped out of the room, and I listened to the banging, now farther away. Sleep faded. There was no danger, no broken glass, no war. My mind cleared, and I wondered at the way my dreams had in an instant transformed clanging pots into mortal peril. In the villages, I'd been told, boys are honored to get up even before the early-morning Call to Prayer so they can bang drums or metal pots to wake up the faithful. And, in this case, the infidel staying among them.

As I stepped into the hallway, bleary-eyed, Maisa was in the bathroom with the door open, splashing water on her face, sweeping a wet finger over her nose, her ears. She had to be ritually clean before she could pray.

I leaned against the doorway while Maisa went to the living room and unrolled a prayer rug. She still had her nightgown on, but it didn't cover enough. Maisa drew an elastic-waisted white skirt up over her pajamas, folding the waistband twice to get the length right. She wrapped her head, arms, and upper body in the other half of the prayer garment so she was shrouded, bowing and rising, facing south to Mecca and then touching her forehead to the prayer rug. When she finished praying, Maisa rushed to the kitchen, stepping out of the skirt and handing it to her mother in exchange for a wooden spoon. We were on a countdown to sunrise, everything fast and fuzzy. Maisa's mother cleansed her own face, nose, and ears in the kitchen sink and then went to the living room to pray in the white garment while Maisa stirred something on the stove.

She was heating mashed dried apricots, the gas turned up so high that the blue flame became orange as it licked the edges of the skillet.

"We must hurry," Maisa said, leaving the apricot mash for a moment to hand me a stack of Arabic bread. She scraped the mash into a dish, and I followed her out to the dining area, where the plastic tablecloth was laid out on the floor, spread with plates of pickles, boiled eggs, olives, and hummus.

Three groggy women in wrinkled nightgowns, we ate sitting on the floor where the dining area opened to the living room, a couple of feet from the prayer rug. We chewed and swallowed quickly. Each of us drank a last draught of water, because it was nearly sunrise.

I helped Maisa and her mother clear the dishes to the kitchen—in our morning stupor, my hosts didn't protest—and we left the washing up for daylight. Maisa pulled on her prayer garment again to do the second prayer, the dawn prayer. Outside, to the east, the sun licked the edges of the village: the fasting had begun.

I went back to bed. The sunrise Call to Prayer echoed; it rose and fell in unmeasured rounds. Seven mosques, I thought, and more. From each, the same recording, the same voice—there must have been a dozen of them in that one village, but the recordings weren't synchronized. They came at slightly different times, falling over one another, vocal eddies breaking open the new day.

Perhaps I should have stayed up with Maisa and done my own prayers. I almost threw the covers back, but the bed was warm, and my God did not require it. I would get up in a few minutes; I would pray. But I'm a Christian, I thought. I can pray in bed. So I did—or I meant to. Maybe I dreamed I was praying. At any rate I was asleep when Maisa finished her own prayers and slipped back under the covers in the other bed.

I heard a phantom Call to Prayer in my dreams, lifting me, pressing me back down into my bed. I saw my Muslim friends praying in white shrouds, all of them lined up together, heads to the ground, rising as one, bowing again. The movement stopped. My friends lay still, prostrate, face down, heads pointed to Mecca. I couldn't tell which one was Maisa. Were they asleep? A cold wind lifted the shrouds, and the white fabric billowed over bones, which turned to dust and blew away down the vacant streets of Damascus.

I sat up, awake, not sure where I was. There was some urgency, something wrong, but I couldn't think what. Maisa's white bedclothes rose and fell slightly with her breathing. Only a dream. I slipped out of bed and found my socks. It was daylight out. The bedroom felt dim and stale. Maisa had pulled the curtain shut against the sun, though the window had been bare all night to the Ramadan moon. Yes, my friend was still breathing. It wasn't too late. I didn't have to be tormented by my dreams like Maisa was by hers.

Had I also dreamed the early breakfast—those mashed apricots on flat Arabic bread? Did Maisa really have two sets of prayers so close together before the day even started?

In the dining room, the plastic tablecloth was still spread on the floor, bread crumbs and a smear of apricot on it to prove that we really had eaten there before dawn.

And Faulkner was there on the chair, over near the prayer rug. The rug looked like that magic carpet of childhood fairy tales, a means of transport to adventures beyond. In the bright morning sun, the carpet showed faded sections where the threads were worn weak by years of knees and foreheads. And on the rug, like grave cloths abandoned, a slump of white fabric: the prayer garment.

A dog barked. I went to the window and saw it, a filthy wild creature from the desert, scrawny, a scavenger hiding from the sun on the shady side of the street. That dog would be gone soon, I knew, back to the dark places where wild things sleep during the day.

The skyline bowed to the sun whose fire burst full and blinding above the rooftops of the village, heaping light in the empty alleys and courtyards. Ascending like a king in a golden chariot the sun advanced, triumphant. The mosque spires appeared to reach higher—but in another hour the sun would soar far above every manmade tower. I opened wide the window to my friend's home to let in the rushing breeze and welcome the sunlight.

CHAPTER 7

TORN VEIL

"Carry them with you," Miriam whispered.

We slipped our shoes off inside the entryway where a jumble of plastic sandals lay on the ground. In the open courtyard pigeons clustered with light rustling of wings, so that even the creatures seemed to hush in reverence.

Miriam helped me arrange the black robe over my shoulders and head. I'd worn a scarf but hadn't thought to wear long sleeves, so the attendant loaned me a wad of fabric that unfolded into a hooded robe. Every other woman visiting the mosque that day wore her own street clothes. I tried to blend in, but somehow I always missed Islamic propriety by an inch of sleeve or the slip of a scarf. The borrowed robe singled me out as the foreigner, the outsider. Instead of covering and equalizing, the black fabric exposed me. I was not a Muslim.

In bare feet we followed the cold tile corridor to the mausoleum where it is said the martyr's bones lie enshrined. The only furnishing in that vast room was Saida Zainab's tomb. It stood like a great throne in the sweeping hall where icy white and blue tiles covered the many arches, walls, and supporting pillars. Chandeliers hung from the high domed ceiling. Steel grillwork made up four sides of the structure, as large as a Bedouin tent, and a lone worshiper stood next to it, a woman wearing an embroidered robe like one of Aaron's priests, her lips moving in silent supplication. Instead of the Ark of the Covenant, she tended a casket. When she reached out to touch its holiness, she did not die.

Loneliness filled the great room and overflowed to blanket the courtyard beneath the open sky, loneliness so heavy it should have split the tiles, broken open the dome. But the mosque walls held.

We settled on the floor a few meters back from the shrine. Miriam placed the soles of her shoes together so they wouldn't touch holy ground, and she tucked them under the fabric of my robe. Across the room a man knelt with his arms wrapped around himself, bowing. Above him a chandelier glittered like a thousand icicles—a thousand and one tiny Damocles' swords.

The day's research topic was firm in my mind—marriage between Sunni and Shia—but I couldn't remember specific questions from the memo pad I carried in my purse. My class leader had only allowed my day trip with a single informant because Miriam was Shia, and we had very few Shia contacts.

The woman at the tomb swayed, her face wet. She held a piece of cloth to her breast, white and clean against her dark clothing. With the cloth in her right hand she leaned against the tomb, kissing the metal grille again and again.

"Why does she do that?" I asked.

"She wants a blessing," Miriam said. "But what she kisses is only silver."

I took out my memo pad to write *blessing* and *only silver;* I flipped pages of field notes to where I'd jotted down research questions based on the previous day's class meeting. Miriam dabbed her nose and eyes with a tissue.

"Today no questions," she said. "No research. Today is for Saida Zainab."

I closed the memo pad—but I would get my notes somehow. The woman at the tomb kissed and polished with silent tears, seeking a blessing. The man under the chandelier bent so far forward that his forehead rested on the ground. Silence filled the mosque and overflowed to the courtyard.

Saida Zainab's shrine walls held tile after tile, the design of every square repeating the one next to it in a silent echo, lonely and lovely.

I think most of the prophets were killed.
—Miriam, Shia university student

The weeping woman pushed one corner of the cloth through the grille surrounding the shrine. She tried to weave the fabric in and out of the metalwork grating.

"She thinks there will be a special power from Saida Zainab in the cloth," Miriam said. "Her life has been hard."

Shias trace their religious heritage through lines of hardship and suffering back to Ali, the prophet Mohammed's cousin and son-in-law. Since Mohammed had no sons and Ali did, it was Ali who carried on the bloodline of the prophet's family and leadership of the new religion— according to Shias. The Sunni branch rejected Ali and followed another line of leaders. So already in the second generation the family of Islam was divided. The Lady Zainab of this shrine was Ali's daughter: like her father, she was assassinated; like her father, Zainab was a martyr.

"She suffered so much," Miriam said. "Our own hardships seem small compared to Saida Zainab's."

I'd read about the self-flagellation on the Day of Ashura and how faithful Shias slash at themselves with whips and knives as a bloody reminder that blood is what ties them to Islam. Ali was the rightful successor to Mohammed, yet he suffered and died. Shias revere suffering. By what conviction do they call down that suffering by cutting and whipping themselves? My own religion is built on a bloody foundation and on suffering, but I have yet to rend my own flesh.

"Through suffering we remember," Miriam said.

I waited to hear what the suffering was, what she remembered. I was ready to memorize her words, to excuse myself to wash hands in the fountain or get a breath of fresh air in the courtyard so I could write some quick research notes. Miriam gave me nothing but silence.

With no new notes coming from my time with Miriam, I would be assigned to seek out a different informant in coming days. If I kept getting key information from my friend, I could continue to count her as an informant and spend a few hours a week with her.

A stray pigeon flew low over the shrine and into the corners of the large room, desperate for a way out. It flapped and flew, as if drunk on loneliness, until it found the wide door. The pigeon landed in the courtyard near a woman and three children seated on the cold tile. The woman untied a piece of cloth, passing bread and boiled eggs to her children.

"They have no other place," Miriam said. "The poor come to Saida Zainab to rest." She spoke as if the martyr were living still. "They are hungry," Miriam said. "Let them eat."

But they would be hungry again.

Would you marry a man who wasn't from Damascus?
Arranged marriage? Marry for love?
—Ethnographic research questions

I met Miriam for the first time at Damascus University, where she was an English major. That first day, leaning against the wall outside a lecture hall, another student told me about a village outside of Damascus. Miriam stood close but didn't speak, even when the other student introduced her as a true Damascene whose grandfather's grandfather had been born there. When the classmate mentioned that Miriam was not Sunni but Shia, I felt a rush of excitement and turned my questions to Miriam, Shia university student. Shifting from small talk to ethnographic interview was becoming second nature to me.

Miriam gave short answers to my questions—yes, no, not sure—and looked past me, as if waiting for someone else. Even if she didn't like me, didn't want to talk with me, I was determined to be the first in my class to bring home field notes from an English-speaking Shia contact.

In English only a few letters differentiate between Sunni and Shia, but for the Muslim there is a world of difference. Presbyterian and Pentecostal understand this. Astronomer and astrologer do, too. From the outside we see Christian, stargazer, Muslim. From the inside, a galaxy separates Sunni from Shia.

Several days later I saw Miriam at the bus station near the university, where we found ourselves waiting for the same bus home. I told her where I lived, with a Syrian Orthodox family in the Old City. "I live not far from you," Miriam said. "Outside the Christian Quarter, nearer the Turkish bath."

My classmates would be impressed. Hidden right under our noses a pocket of Shias lived behind the doors we walked past nearly every day. Questions formed and clicked. How many? Do they intermarry? Is there a Shia mosque nearby?

"Maybe I can visit your home sometime, Miriam. Are your neighbors all Shia, too?"

She narrowed her eyes. Until now my Arab informants had invited me to their homes with no prompting, even upon our first introduction. Perhaps Shias were more distant, self-protective. But Miriam was an Arab, and the pre-Islamic hospitality of her ancestors took over. She welcomed the wayfarer.

"You may come home with me now, today. Meet my mother and sisters."

Miriam lived in the Old City, just five minutes through stone corridors from my own host family. Her doorway looked exactly like every doorway surrounding it, the entry off the street so ancient, so low that we had to duck to enter.

Three years after I said goodbye to Miriam and left Syria I came back to Damascus for a visit. My letters to Miriam had been returned as undeliverable, whether addressed in Arabic or in English. I hoped her family was still there in the Old City. I hoped that Miriam would remember me. But after three years' absence the identical doors set in the stone walls of her lane confused me. I stood under an archway, unsure which door to try first.

An old man selling Pepsi at the corner left his cart and came to the archway. He gestured for me to follow and led me without hesitation. He knocked hard on a door, calling out that she was here—the girl from America had returned.

I didn't remember this old man but he knew who I was and recognized me, even after three years' absence. I felt a sharp ache for my months in Damascus; I wished I'd paid more attention, learned more Arabic. I longed to go back and start over, to remain in Damascus, build a life there. The old man slipped back to his cart when Miriam's mother opened the door and gathered me in her arms with joyful tears of reunion.

Shias always remember.

But on my visit to Miriam's home that first day, her mother hurried to greet me with a warm smile and a large mole on her upper lip. Months later, when I left Damascus, this ugly woman would capture me in an embrace while Miriam translated the words that reminded me of a Flannery O'Connor short story I'd read sophomore year.

"You are my daughter. You are my own child."

Miriam kept her head covered the day she introduced me to her family, though her mother and sisters were unveiled before me. She served me tea but didn't drink. I felt from her a reserve, a distance. Perhaps Miriam would never be a cooperative informant.

Her father joined us for the meal. He greeted me and gestured that I should sit between Miriam and her mother. We sat and ate together as I had with so many Syrian families during my months in Damascus. A good Arab hostess, Miriam scooped more rice and vegetables onto my plate and refilled my drink each time I got it down to the halfway point. But she did not eat.

When the meal ended Miriam's two sisters cleared the dishes and rolled up the mat. Her father leaned back against a bolster, and Miriam brought him a cigarette and matches.

With my memo pad and a short pencil in hand I asked Miriam if she would translate for me. She made eye contact with her father, but he ignored her and looked to me kindly. Miriam chewed her bottom lip a moment before telling me to go ahead with my questions.

He prayed at the Shia mosque near the Street Called Straight, he told me. He liked to visit the nearby Ommayed Mosque where the great martyr John the Baptist's head was enshrined. But the martyr he loved most was the Prophet's granddaughter Zainab, and as an expression of his devotion, he owned a small summer home near her shrine, on the outskirts of Damascus.

When I saw Miriam again she smiled at me with her mother's warm smile. As we walked through campus she linked her arm in mine. We found a splintery wooden bench and sat together while students rushed past us, most turning to gape at the foreigner. Miriam looked right at me as she spoke. She promised to teach me many things, to help me with my research, she said. Her father wanted me to know that I was welcome in his home every day, as one of his own children.

Miriam became my closest friend in Damascus. She eventually told me that her early distance was because she feared that I was a spy. The memo pad and questions made Miriam suspicious and frightened. Her father laughed at Miriam's fears and was happy to answer my questions. Was your wife from Damascus? Are all of your family friends Damascenes? Would you let your daughters make friends with a Palestinian girl? With a villager? *These,* he told Miriam, *were not the sorts of questions that a spy would ask. A spy would likely keep her memo pad hidden. A spy would be more clever than you, daughter. You would never suspect her. This one is not a spy. She is your friend.*

In Paradise we will drink from cups of gold.
We'll have better clothes than we ever had here.
I hope to see you in heaven with me, and not in hell.
Inshallah, I will be there.
—Miriam, Shia university student

I handed the black robe back to the attendant and slipped on my shoes. Her parents were already in the small house a few minutes' walk from the mosque, Miriam said. Her mother had carried in minced lamb for kabob; we would have a small holiday. An Arab lunch would stretch out my afternoon, and still I had no answers to my day's research questions. It wasn't right for me to stay and socialize when I hadn't finished my ethnographic work for the day.

In a few hours my classmates would all gather to compare and discuss their field notes. There would be time for me to do a couple of interviews once I got back to Damascus if I caught a bus right away. I'd need to say hello to Miriam's parents and then excuse myself. Return to Damascus, contact new informants, and make up for my wasted morning. I would redeem the day.

"Just come," Miriam said.

We walked into the courtyard and the fragrance of roasted meat rose to welcome us. Miriam's mother stepped around the fountain to greet me with a kiss. "Welcome, my daughters. You must eat." I was an ancient desert traveler, thirsty and hungry, in need of shelter. My hosts had killed the fattened calf.

The meal was set up on the ground beside the courtyard fountain. Miriam's father turned a spigot and the water splashed over the tiles the way a late summer rain in the desert plops and spatters over the parched earth. I wouldn't stay for long, but I could take time for the ones who called me daughter.

Miriam took up the aluminum water pitcher, pouring into the glass an echo of the sprinkling fountain behind us. Her mother knelt beside me and tore a piece of bread, ripped off a sprig of fresh herbs, and reached for the meat piled on a large round of bread before us. "Good health," she said, handing me the wrap of bread, meat, and herbs.

Miriam's father echoed the blessing, "Good health." And so they ministered to the stranger and sojourner, feeding me as one of their own. We ate together from that common loaf, all of us tearing hunks of bread and reaching for the meat and herbs.

Miriam poured water into the glass we would share. She held it out so I could drink first then refilled it and drank after me. After the meal Miriam's mother and father retreated to one of the rooms that opened to the courtyard. Her father came out only to pull an extra mat into the other room for us.

"And now we will rest," said Miriam.

I imagined my classmates walking through hot streets in Damascus, finding informants, taking notes. I had nothing to show for my day, nothing to type up on a laptop that evening when the rest of my class would scurry to claim a computer and organize their notes into research topics. I would return from Saida Zainab empty-handed.

But my Shia hosts had filled me and I was sleepy. To honor them I must rest. Research questions written across my closed eyelids stretched and drifted to the sound of the rain. Not rain—it was the fountain, baptizing the tiles, washing away the sand and dust. The sound filled the open courtyard and overflowed into the room where we rested,

Miriam on one mat and I on another. It washed away my questions and thoughts of bus schedules back to Damascus. It lifted me to the place of trust and sleep.

Miriam shook me awake. "Come with me."

Disoriented from the nap, I followed her out into the courtyard, where she handed me a thick cloth, her face as solemn as a priest's. She showed me how to fold the cloth over the handle of a steaming teapot so I could lift it without burning myself. Miriam took up a scratched metal tray with two small, clear glasses and a bowl of sugar. A scarf was drawn over her head loosely with the ends untied and hanging from her temples like the long prayer curls I'd seen on Jewish worshipers.

We formed a two-woman procession across the courtyard, past the fountain where streams of water still flowed and splashed, sprinkling us as we passed. The drops made her face shine in the sunlight as she balanced the tray on her right hand to take hold of the wooden ladder that led to the roof. I climbed the wooden ladder after her, the teapot swinging in my hand, steam rising from it as if from a golden censer.

Once we had ascended to the rooftop Miriam set the tray on a small platform made of several tile blocks stacked together. I set the hot teapot directly on the stone table, and we removed our shoes.

Overhead the sky formed a blue dome with the sun as its warm and brilliant chandelier. A breeze lifted my hair and teased at Miriam's loose scarf until she let it fall from her head. There were no men on surrounding rooftops to see the private glory of her hair.

Miriam confessed her secrets to me that afternoon, things she hadn't told anyone, not even her mother. There was a man, she told me, a gentle man. "Not a cousin, but he is good. If God wills, he will talk to my father. If God wills, he will come for me."

And she told me of growing up in Damascus and attending an Islamic school for girls, where a classmate became her best friend. She was like a sister, the friend Miriam had hoped and waited for. Miriam told her friend a family secret and found relief in sharing the burden of it—until she came home one afternoon to find her mother beating carpets and crying, her face dirty and wretched.

"We must not trust them, my daughter. The scorpion hides in walls and on rooftops. If you do not look around before you step, she will bite you."

There in Damascus, the city of their birth, their language, their religion—surrounded by households long established alongside their own—Miriam's family was alone. They smiled at neighbors when they passed them on the lane, but they did not reach out in friendship. It is foolish to befriend a scorpion or a neighbor. Not one could be trusted.

"Even my brother's wife is not one of us," Miriam said. "A good friend would be trustworthy and true. I long for such a friend."

Miriam took up the teapot and before pouring she said the Arabic blessing: In the name of God the merciful and compassionate. She tipped two small spoonfuls of sugar into each glass and stirred until the sugar dissolved, softening the tannic bite of the tea. It is the tannin in tea that brings relaxation, I've read. Drink the bitter tannin and you'll rest better. Red wine has tannin and it's that bitterness that finishes the wine. So take and drink. Enter into your rest.

Out beyond the rooftops of the neighborhood rose the mosque's golden dome and elaborate tiled minarets. The gold rotunda shone like Jerusalem's Dome of the Rock, reflecting the sun, glowing over the poor dusty surroundings. The dome burned my eyes and I couldn't look directly at it, even though, like the Ramadan moon, the mosque had no light of its own.

We sipped the tea together. Miriam told me about the hollow ache she felt when the heat of summer left the stone walls of the Old City each October, making way for chilled days, rain, and sometimes snow falling directly into the courtyard. She described her longing for the days of her childhood when marriage was something that would someday enfold her and draw her into the kindness of another family. That was before she had suffered. Before she had trusted, before she had tried love and found it wanting.

She would never again allow her heart to love until she was engaged, maybe not until marriage. There was too much pain—no certainty that love would be returned. Just as she wouldn't be sure that Allah would let her into Paradise until he made his choice on the Day of Judgment, she would not be sure of a man's love until she was his bride.

Miriam knew the pain of love without promise. This was her suffering. She had been left alone. Until now she held up a veil between her words and her heart, but our friendship had torn the partition down. Why had she chosen to reveal herself? We both knew that I, too, would betray her. In a few weeks my study tour would be over and I would leave Damascus. I wrote nothing in my memo pad that afternoon, though she answered every question. I knew I would remember.

When I would return to Damascus those few years later, Miriam would be married to a good man, a gentle man, a poor man. She would have a son and be called

Mother of Hamood. She would live in the Old City, a lane away from the family home. She would serve her husband meat once a week—lentils and tomatoes and brown beans the other days. And this man would love her. With him she would suffer in poverty, with a son and a daughter and conversation on cold nights and someone to trust until death separates. Still, she would feel the longing for something more.

Every year the Ramadan moon grows full over Damascus and then diminishes. Near the end of the month of fasting the dim light of the aging moon holds its veil over the city. Since childhood Miriam has gone to the roof of her Old City home on that particular night to remember how the Koran was given, to remember that night when Allah revealed and Allah spoke. She knows that Allah does not condescend to come down, yet she aches to know and be known.

On this night the veiled moon gives enough light for Miriam to grasp the wooden ladder, holding her Koran in her right hand, wrapped in a white cloth. Alone on the rooftop she unwraps the Koran, kisses it, presses it to her forehead, and opens it to read.

Across the Old City rooftops she sees the minarets rising from the big mosque that holds a shrine for John the Baptist. The southwestern spire is the Minaret of Jesus, where Damascenes say that the Prophet Jesus will first alight on the great Day of Judgment.

She wants a blessing and she will return to the rooftop year after year on this Night of Revelation, patient and hopeful and lonely. Miriam watches and waits for morning to split the sky from east to west. She watches for the veil to be torn, for the heavens to fall.

CHAPTER 8

CHILD OF THE PAST

Afternoon II

The tile courtyard lay torn to rubble at our feet. Pieces of the cement fountain were chunked against the walls of the house.

"What's going on here?" my husband asked.

Abu Moosa spoke with such excitement—and half in Arabic. We couldn't understand. Renovations? Where did he get the money? Abu Moosa proudly pointed out features of the broken stones. We saw but didn't understand. In those days, three years after our study tour in Damascus, we couldn't tell Byzantine from Mamluk, couldn't tell rubble from sherds.

Damascus is built over ruins. When floors are demolished in some Old City homes, archeologists are called in to exhume the Roman architecture lying beneath the ground floor. Ruins lie eight feet under the ancient lanes of the Old City. We touched history as we ducked under archways and walked alongside the same stone walls that generations of Syrian boys dragged sticks across, bump bumping at each joint of stone. History is layered under history. We knew so little. Who built these walls? What former cultures were lost when the conquerors built right over the ruins of what had gone before? In Damascus, without knowing it, we walked on mystery.

Afternoon I

Todd and I had been married just two years when we returned to touch the past and to reach toward the future, to visit Syrian friends from our student days and to see what prospects Damascus held for serious language study, perhaps teaching English, for starting a family.

One stop on our pilgrimage was the falafel stand near Abu Moosa's house. The brothers who had run the shop during our study tour still worked there—three years of mashing chick peas, scooping them into patties, and dropping them in boiling oil. Their business must have prospered. The brothers dressed in nicer clothing, moved at a less frantic pace. The line was long at the falafel stand that afternoon but the brothers recognized us right away and stepped out into the lane to shake Todd's hand and to let me take their picture.

That photo is stored in a box along with one taken three years earlier. In the first photo, the brothers look harried, wearing worn shirts and stained slacks. Three years later they are relaxed and happy in stylish shirts tucked into crisp trousers.

Unlike other tourists in Damascus, we glimpsed the past when we looked at these brothers and their success. We remembered, as their neighbors did, the earlier days of this business, these brothers. We skimmed the surface of the present, dipped into the shallows, but we didn't fathom the depths. Neighbors standing in line with us must have remembered when these young men kicked a soccer ball down the dusty lanes of the neighborhood with the other boys, how they scrapped with each other, how no one thought they'd make it in business together.

An Arabic proverb says *you are the child of your past.*

It takes time to know and to be known. In a city like Damascus there's a depth of knowing that my modern nomadic life lacks.

After taking the brothers' picture Todd and I stood eating our falafel sandwiches, watching the people in line as they watched us. One of them was blue-eyed Abu Moosa, our Damascus landlord.

Abu Moosa gave up his place in line and reached up to grab Todd's face, kissing him on both cheeks. He took Todd by the hand and pulled him down the lane, talking quickly in Arabic and broken English. Renovations? What could he mean? I followed after them, toward our old home.

Morning

Diesel fumes mixed with the aroma of fresh-baked bread as the heat of the day descended. I wore a skirt, long-sleeved blouse, and scarf. Todd wore slacks despite the heat. Friends back home had assumed that Todd's dark hair and beard helped him to blend into crowds in the Middle East. It went without saying that my fair hair would make me stand out—but we lived out the opposite of our friends' expectations. Our first day back in Damascus I snapped a picture of Todd crossing a busy street. I wanted the photo to show why he didn't blend into a crowd of Arabs even when dressed like one. He stood a head taller than the slight men who leaned forward as they crossed the street, one or two lifting their heads to stare at the foreign man. No one stared at me. This time I knew to pack long skirts, long sleeves, low pumps, and scarves. I stood back and let Todd do the talking. When the man at the juice stand asked Todd if I was Syrian, I was delighted.

In my student days in Damascus, three years earlier, I wore all the wrong clothes. My loose dresses hung to mid-calf, short sleeved for the heat but immodest for Islam. Syrian friends wore straight pencil skirts with stylish, long-sleeved blouses. How could I have known? When I packed for the study tour, I had two things in mind: heat and modesty. I'd have done better to bring money and shop in Syria. I wore out my American shoes in the first six weeks trekking on cobblestone and cement. While window-shopping for shoes, I snickered at the fussy bows and sprays of netting that adorned women's everyday pumps. Maybe for a special occasion, but all this froof for everyday wear? The shoes I bought were simple by Syrian standards. Suede pumps in charcoal gray with a floral pattern pressed into the leather. Syrian shoes bore bows that season, and on these shoes, too, perched neat bows of charcoal suede. I thought of buying a fussy white pair, to save them for my wedding day. But there was no man in my life—or so I thought—and I didn't want to presume that providence would bring me one.

When I married Todd I wore a tea-length dress with a white floral pattern overprinted on the white cotton. The back of the dress plunged to mid-back where a neat bow perched. My wedding shoes were low and plain and cost about three times what I would have paid for an embellished pair of white pumps in Damascus. Who can tell the future? We only know the past.

Midnight

Our flight arrived after midnight and with our one suitcase and two backpacks Todd and I boarded the last bus from the airport into downtown Damascus. It was three days until our second anniversary.

We walked the dark streets like Mary and Joseph, turning away from hotel after hotel. There were vacancies, but we knew the prices being asked for dirty beds and a shared bathroom were too high. We kept trying the next hotel and the next. Downtown Damascus was unfamiliar in the moonlight and without crowds. Finally we surrendered and paid too high a price. Sleep took Todd immediately but I was hyper-awake, sensitive to every sound, every possibility. Reunited to the city I had loved and longed for, I lay awake remembering my student days in Damascus. Who needs sleep or food when she's in love?

Student Days

"Todd, this is so awkward. I'm just not interested in you that way."

"Never thought you were. Good friends is all."

"Okay then. It felt like maybe there was something new."

"Nope. Nothing like that."

We stood in comfortable silence, looking out over the rooftops of Damascus. In six months I would tell Todd my feelings had changed. A little over a year later we would be married. In three years we would be back here in Damascus together, peering at Abu Moosa's demolished courtyard, blind to the deeper past spread before us under a layer of dust.

Into the Past

I met Todd the first day of training for our ethnographic research project. He was tall and bearded and looked like an intellectual with his perfectly round John Lennon glasses. I knew who he was. I walked up behind him in the lunch line, stuck out my hand and said, "I'm Kyle's friend from Oregon. You must be Todd Harris."

Kyle came back to town the summer I graduated from college, but he didn't come back to see graduation. He came back to marry Becky. That summer I lived in an old sorority-style co-op just off campus. Kyle and Becky dropped by one day and I told them of my plans to go on a study tour in a few months.

"Two tours, right? One to Syria and one to Turkey?"

How did Kyle know?

"I know a guy from Indiana who's going on that," Kyle said. "Todd Harris. Interested in the Middle East. A great guy."

Great guy? Middle East? Going on my study tour? I had always been susceptible to romantic hopes, and my heart leapt.

"Yeah, but he's got a girlfriend." Kyle knew me.

I wasn't nervous or hopeful when I met Todd. I wasn't thinking romance. He had a girlfriend back home—a girl not interested in the Middle East, not interested in urban life or many of the things Todd held dear. Things that drew me just as they drew him. By the time I fell in love with Todd, he was already my best friend. We built romantic love over the shared history of a solid friendship, and the structure has held.

Chunks of memory and fragments of connection lie pushed up against the corners of my past and Todd's. How many can be traced? As children, our families visited Yellowstone National Park the same summer. We don't recall, nor do our parents or siblings, what month, which dates we were there. It's utterly fantastical to speculate whether our paths crossed before we were aware of one another. What are the chances? But what are the chances my friend Kyle would go to grad school halfway across the country and there become friends with the man I would marry?

I lie awake sometimes beside Todd, listening to his even breathing, and I trace back in time to find what first stone laid the foundation for all of this—for Damascus, for my marriage. We both loved the Middle East. For me, it started because I glimpsed a world outside of America. I go back as far into memory as I can. When did I first learn about the Arab world, about Islam and the Middle East?

Her name was Nadia. It started with a pen pal from Saudi Arabia.

CHAPTER 9

TELL SOME SECRETS

Dear Nadia,
It's snowing as I write this letter and I'm trying to imagine how it would look through your eyes. Like feathers floating down. Like salt and pepper from a giant shaker. The snow makes everything look new and perfect.

Dear Lisa,
It's Ramadan again. I love how everyone is kind even though we're hungry and thirsty all day. Fasting helps us know how the poor feel, and we feel sad but also thankful. Even the person who is usually mean becomes tender during Ramadan. I wish the world could be like this always.

Dear Nadia,
I have my first summer job. I work for a small farm and we just finished picking strawberries. Raspberries come next, and then blackberries. My dad is even thinking about putting in a couple of acres of berries on our place next spring.

Dear Lisa,
We're in Bombay for the summer again. It's not as
boring as Saudi because I can get out of the house
whenever. But I'm lonely. I wish you could spend
the summer with me in India.

Nadia's letters crinkled on thin paper. I imagined a
sandstorm stippling my windows as I pulled photographs
from between thin onionskin pages. In our preteen years
when we were matched as pen pals Nadia's photos showed
a girl with curly black hair and deep eyes, sometimes smiling, usually looking off to the side of the camera. Through
high school and especially as we neared graduation Nadia's pictures more often had her head covered, once with a
black and white checkered Palestinian scarf wrapped over
her curls like a turban.

Dear Lisa,
We must meet soon. I will ask my father. You ask
yours.

I daydreamed about Saudi Arabia. Mom said I would
have to put on a huge black veil as soon as I got off the airplane. I pictured the black cloth flapping in desert siroccos
as I descended onto the tarmac. Nadia would be waiting
there, scarf billowing away from her face. I would run to
her like an old friend.

We planted in March. Dad plunged the shovel into the
ground and threw his weight against the handle to open
the earth. Into the wound I laid the root end. Mom held

the cane straight while Dad and I tamped down the soil all around. Then Dad stood tall, swung his right leg and took a long step down the row to slice open the earth and plant the next cane a man's stride from the last.

After Easter we mulched each row to conserve the soil's moisture when the rains dispersed in late spring. Raspberries must be kept moist the first year, and we had no irrigation system. The last two weeks of June Dad inspected the green plants and the soil around them every few days, until he announced that they needed watering.

"Will we have berries soon, Dad?"

"We might. But probably not until the second year. And only if we take good care of them."

I hauled the long garden hose across the driveway and front lawn, then snaked it through the landscaping under the crabapple trees to reach out to the raspberry field. I let the hose lie with water running slowly down the length of each row until thirty minutes or an hour later, when I shifted the hose to a new position.

By July the raspberry canes had multiplied, sending runners up and down the rows. I didn't mind standing out in the field to hand water them. It gave me a way to pass the long days and an excuse to daydream. The August sun was so hot and bright that I borrowed one of Dad's caps. I imagined myself controlling rain clouds over a lonely desert land where my sparkling rain brought relief and blessing.

Dear Lisa,
My family is coming to America—to Disneyland. I'll call you when we arrive. Can you hop on a bus to Anaheim and meet me there?

Mom and I laughed that Nadia thought Anaheim was a short bus ride from Oregon. "She's about to find out how big America is," Mom said.

When Nadia called, my stomach jumped and tingled. She spoke with a light British accent. She wanted me to meet up with her. "Can't you ask your boyfriend to drive you or something?"

"I have to work. I'm saving for college. It's a long trip."

"I will talk to my father."

When the phone rang again Nadia said in her British accent, "We are coming to you. Can your boyfriend bring you to Portland?"

My parents drove me the two hours to Portland, to the hotel where Nadia and her family stayed. They had driven a rental car sixteen hours one way, just so Nadia and I could meet.

"Wear a dress," my mother advised me. "We want to be sure not to offend Nadia or her family."

Though I've been away from the Pacific Northwest for years now, the raspberries I remember are deep red. When ripe their fruit is both tart and sweet. They are of the genus *Rubus,* which makes me think of rubies. But not all Rubus berries are red.

Raspberries come in a variety of colors worldwide, red and yellow, black and albino. The colors of the berries have much to do with the climate they're grown in. Northern Indian raspberries are black, while European raspberries are fair, yellow and white. The red-skinned raspberry, native to North America, has the sweetest berries of any Rubus species.

These berries are delicate and must be picked into shallow trays lest they crush the fruit layered beneath. I see raspberries in the grocery stores these days though I have seldom purchased them. It's hard to bring myself to pay dearly for what was once free for the picking. When I do the result is disappointing. Those store-bought and sterile tasting, slightly moldy berries evoke little nostalgia for me. Instead I will savor the memory of a sun-warmed raspberry bursting seedy between my teeth. I'll fast from raspberries until I can return to the Northwest and search them out once again. No substitute will do.

I'd made assumptions about Nadia as a repressed Muslim woman just as she'd made assumptions—like the boyfriend—about American me. I expected her to be veiled. I expected her father to be stern and controlling, her mother covered and cowering. When we entered the hotel restaurant an American-looking family waved to us, curly haired Nadia jumping out of the booth and running to embrace me, as in my fantasy only without the veil. She wore blue jeans and a T-shirt. Nadia kissed me on both cheeks then embraced and kissed my mother. Her father shook hands with mine and ushered my parents into the booth where he and his wife sat over coffee and Belgian waffles.

"You girls go for a walk," Nadia's dad said. "We don't need to hear your secrets." Our parents laughed companionably as we walked out of the hotel restaurant into the parking lot.

"Well, I guess we'd better walk," Nadia said. "And tell some secrets. Come on."

It was so much easier than writing. We walked behind the hotel where a wooded area backed the parking lot, Douglas fir trees bunched in a tight mass of wilderness at the sunny edge of the asphalt.

"What's that sound?" Nadia asked.

I listened to hear what she heard. "It's the wind blowing through the branches."

"Sounds like water doesn't it?"

"Yeah, but it's the wind."

Nadia lifted her head to see the tops of the trees.

"I'm going to be a doctor someday," she said. "To help poor people. And you?"

I had no plans beyond the first semester of classes. No idea that I'd end up working with ESL students my last two years of college and then for a while after graduation. No idea that I would travel the world and study Arabic and wear a veil myself.

The first year of cultivation the canes grow leaves and send out runners. In the second year they will flower and bear fruit, then die. To maximize fruit production, canes must not be allowed to grow too close together.

Raspberry bushes bear fruit only every other year. The inexperienced grower may pull out canes in the year they don't produce, destroying in one quick tug all possibilities for future fruit.

"You should come with us," Nadia said. "We're going to see Yellowstone and the Grand Canyon. My father will take care of you. We'll take you shopping, get what you need for the trip."

"I have to work," I told Nadia. "I can't quit my summer job and take off traveling just like that."

"Why not?" Nadia asked.

"I don't know. But I can't."

Halfway home from Portland I told my parents about it, expecting to share a laugh with Mom about how little Nadia knew about summer jobs and travel plans.

"She invited me to hop in their car and go to the Grand Canyon."

Dad and Mom exchanged a look.

"Oh, honey. You should have asked us. What an opportunity,"

The air conditioning in the car suddenly felt too cold. As Dad drove us south Nadia's family would have checked out of the hotel and driven east along the Columbia River Gorge, an empty seat in the rental car where I could have been. When they stopped at a scenic overlook, Nadia would explain to her family that the sound like rushing water was actually the wind blowing through the treetops. Without me there to tell them, they wouldn't know that the way the Columbia River cut through the gorge looked exactly like the way water from our garden hose found the path of least resistance through the soil at the base of our raspberry rows.

The red raspberry plant, *Rubus idaeus,* produces a tart, sweet, red fruit in early summer. Though it is called a berry it is not a proper berry at all, but a fruit formed of many smaller parts, called drupelets, clustered around a central core.

With many berry varieties the central core is part of the fruit. Pick a blackberry and the core comes away from the bush to be eaten, soft and tasty, along with the fruit. But the raspberry, when picked, separates from its core. The core then remains on the vine, leaving the cap of fruit hollow.

We lost touch sometime during our college years, Nadia busy with medical school, me always changing addresses and working to pay for college. If we'd persevered with stamps and onionskin paper just a few years longer we could have switched to email to exchange news of weddings and babies and travels. When I lived in the Middle East we might have arranged a rendezvous. Or perhaps I would have said no to Nadia again. Perhaps she would have known me so well by then that she wouldn't have bothered asking.

Every year or so I look for Nadia on the Internet. This year I found her name in the caption of a photograph. I easily picked her face out of the group. No link to an email address for her, but at least I know she's still living. In another year or two, as the Internet braids more and more information together, there will be a way for me to contact Nadia. While I wait and hope for the future, I excavate the past to find indications of what we shall yet be in what we once were.

Dear Nadia,
I remember the crinkling of onionskin paper as I look at your face in this picture online. You stand

with a delegation of doctors traveling to Central Asia. Your head is uncovered, and a red ribbon holds your curls back from your face. You are a doctor now. You help the poor.

We must meet soon. We'll drink a tall latte or share a squat demitasse of Arabic coffee. We'll fly through memories of the years since college, where I've been and where you've been, until we catch up to the present. We'll cultivate the friendship long neglected; we'll savor its remaining fruit.

"I wish you didn't have to go," Nadia said as we circled the hotel yet again. "It's so nice here."

"I know," I said, surprised. "A hotel parking lot, but it feels like we're in a different world."

"I wish we could stay here forever," she said. We listened to the wind in the trees.

"Hey look! Nadia, see over there? Those are raspberry bushes." In a sunny area we found them, the wild canes tall and prickly, hairy leaves stretching out like protective umbrellas over the clusters of red berries. The berries slipped off the caps and we ate mouthfuls, perfectly ripe and sun-warmed, bursting seedy between our teeth, with just the right combination of tart and sweet.

CHAPTER 10

FIRST PRAYER

The swirling Call to Prayer blasted from a Jordanian mosque across the street from our hotel. Too loud. Still dark outside. Would it be like this every day for the next three months? My roommates stirred, getting out of bed in the dark, moving to the window of our room. When it was light, after we'd had breakfast, we would travel together by bus, north to the Syrian border and on to Damascus.

I joined my roommates at the window and in the light of a streetlight we watched two men roll out prayer rugs in the parking lot and pray the same Muslim prayers their ancestors have prayed for centuries.

The hotel faced the main bus station in Amman, Jordan, just down from the blue King Abdullah Mosque. My roommates went back to bed as the Call to Prayer ended. I looked out the window and wished I could take a walk on the vacant street. I didn't dare. This was the scary Middle East where I'd been told I would need to dye my hair brown and not venture out alone after dark. Those warnings would prove completely wrong—I would enjoy great safety and freedom in Damascus. Whoever told me to dye my hair had never lived in this part of the Middle East.

I stayed in my hotel room and watched the sky grow lighter and lighter above the hills of Amman. The guide-book I carried with me said that Amman was originally built on seven hills and had been but a village until 1948, when thousands of Palestinians sought refuge—and eventually, citizenship—in Jordan. Their numbers increased even more after the 1967 war. In 1990 Palestinians who had settled in Kuwait fled to Jordan. Iraqis were soon added to the refugee count. Amman continues to extend outward with a growing population. Now it's a city of over two million.

Six years later I would myself be counted among the population of Amman as a resident alien. From my own rooftop I would watch Amman's changing skyline through the seasons of our first year of Arabic studies—exploring her downtown streets, shopping away from the tourists, and speaking Arabic with my neighbors. Two of my own babies would be born in Amman.

If I could have seen the future as I looked out that window I would have seen myself trudging up that same street six, seven, eight years in the future with one, two, then three daughters in tow. Amman would be my home as a new mother learning to heat water on the stove for my baby's bath our first winter in Jordan. As a language student I would sit in front of a space heater by winter offering my language helper the same hot sugared tea she would drink with me a few months later on our balcony, water dumped onto the tile floor to cool our feet as it evaporated into the dry summer air.

Damascus was my first love but it was Amman that became my home. As a single woman in Damascus I had no concerns outside of my research and my friends. If in Damascus I was a child, Amman saw me through to my womanhood.

Todd also woke at that first Call to Prayer in Amman. He slept in the hotel room next door to mine. And he stayed up to watch the beginning of that first day. At the time, neither of us knew the other was awake, each watching the sky lighten, each wondering about the future. We were married for more than ten years before Todd read these words and told me he'd also stayed awake when his roommate went back to sleep.

An Arab boy trudged up the street. He stopped under my window and pounded on the door a floor below me; he called out in Arabic and pounded again. I pulled back, breathing fast. Had he seen my outline in the window? As I so often would during my years in the Middle East, I imagined drama where there was none.

While I was afraid to be a woman leaving her hotel room unaccompanied in the dangerous Middle East, Todd gave no thought to rising and going down alone to the scroungy lobby on the first floor. When that boy pounded on the hotel's glass door and hollered at Todd in Arabic, Todd just sat and watched him. The boy shook his fist at Todd and walked away.

As the sun rose over Amman, Todd watched the waking streets of the city. He nodded to the hotel manager who came to unlock the door for a morning delivery. One floor up, I tied a scarf over my hair and hoisted my suitcase, eager to leave Amman and cross the Syrian border and head up to Damascus. I was oblivious to the bold strokes of foreshadowing that were being written into my own life's story.

CHAPTER 11

O Barren One

"A thousand and one treatments," Leila said. "All right here in Jordan. Shots and pills, month after month, until finally Allah gave us success."

Leila's heavy eyebrows made her look perpetually troubled. Small vertical wrinkles between her brows added to the effect. I drank black tea, thick with sugar, but Leila sipped only water from a small glass. Her blood pressure had been a bit high the last time she'd visited the obstetrician.

"Allah is gracious. But my sister-in-law still has no child—"

The door opened and Amira joined us, winking at me and dropping a plastic sack onto the coffee table as she sat down. I'd hoped Amira would come. She was the one I wanted for my best friend, the one who would help me with my Arabic studies and show me how to dress and stand and walk so that I belonged. Amira's eyes met mine; she liked me, too.

When Leila reached for the teapot she groaned, pressing her lower back with the other hand. Amira swatted playfully at her grumpy sister-in-law's hand, and then she poured and sugared her own tea.

"It feels like a camel is biting my back," said Leila. "Nothing helps."

Backache, sleep problems, touchy bladder, indigestion. Leila had endured the years of newlywed shame and then the fertility treatments. Now her list of pregnancy complaints was a comfort to all of us, proclaiming that she was no longer a barren woman.

Amira dumped the contents of her sack out on the coffee table: drinking straws, scissors, string, and metallic-looking wrapping paper printed with floral designs—the same material they make balloons of back in the States. In a land of sand and stone, synthetic wrapping is cheaper than that made of tree pulp. The sheets of reflective paper had the glimmer of an oasis, of a dark desert sky full of stars, of jewelry in the bazaar, of the sun shining off the brass ornaments on a camel's saddle in the distance. All the sparkling promises of something good on the way.

"And how is the baby today, O my sister?"

"He pushes and kicks," Leila answered. "He wants to be sure a cousin doesn't arrive before he does."

Amira smiled as she picked up scissors and cut flowers from the reflective paper. There was no child in her womb to vie for position with Leila's baby.

Because Leila's husband was the firstborn son he and Leila lived on the second floor, in the place of honor above his parents' home on the ground floor. Like so many of our neighbors outside of Amman, the extended family lived in a building made up of family apartments. The patriarch and his wife had the first-floor apartment, where the foundation of the family formed the foundation of the home. Apartments rose to accommodate a new floor for each married son.

Amira's husband was the younger brother so she lived on the third floor, climbing more stairs than Leila to reach the place where she could shed her scarf and relax. Dark makeup lined her round, hazel eyes. Gold jewelry flashed on her fingers—rings and bracelets proclaimed her husband's love for her despite their childlessness. Amira and her husband, married three years now, had finally started their own fertility treatments.

She was always cheerful, which was probably why I wanted her for my closest friend rather than Leila. Amira was light and laughter to Leila's shadow and grumbling. When I think about it now, I often felt gloomy myself in those early months. Perhaps in Leila I saw too close a mirror of myself. In Amira I saw who I hoped to be—a woman cheerful in the face of discouragement, rather than one who found fault in every blessing.

Amira stacked the flower cutouts and used the sharp end of her scissors to pierce their centers. She slipped the cord through a length of drinking straw and threaded it through the hole in each metallic flower. Then another length of straw, to form a strand of what would become something like the bead curtain of a college dorm room. Amira intended to hang it in her bedroom on one side of the marriage bed.

Childlessness is seldom a choice in Arab culture. Fertility and infertility are ghosts in the cultural air. A bride on her wedding day is ruffled and jeweled, her face smooth and perfect with a layer of makeup as thick as oil paint on a portrait. Within weeks of the "night of entry" female relatives watch for signs of morning sickness. Every bride hopes for a timely pregnancy and birth—a son, if Allah wills. During the years Todd and I lived in the Middle East I became pregnant twice and gave birth both times to daughters. My Arab friends comforted me, saying that Allah would surely give me a son the next time. A daughter opens the womb for her future brothers.

On the vacant hillside lot across the lane from our apartment, scrubby little boys played before and after school. Without balls or toy trucks to share between them, the boys of our neighborhood threw stones or tossed plastic shopping bags in the air to catch the wind like stringless kites. It took me a while to realize that I never saw little girls play on the streets or in the vacant lots. Grumpy Leila told me that little girls were most likely helping with the work of the home while their brothers played outside.

Amira gathered a stack of the flower cutouts in her palm and lifted them before Leila like an offering. Then Amira blew on her palm, and the flowers showered Leila's lap. We laughed.

"Wife of my husband's brother," Leila said. "May children bow at your feet."

"Children are better than gold," Amira agreed.

When female relatives visited the household they used to greet Amira with kisses and reach for her abdomen to see if a bump was growing. But years had passed. Now the female relatives called her barren.

Amira spent her wedding night there in the same building as her in-laws, grafted into the family that very first night. The guests cheered as Amira and her husband retreated upstairs. In nine months, they said, she will bring us a son and we will enlarge the tent for him.

How different my life was from an Arab woman's, though I tried hard to blend in. I wasn't part of anything larger than my own marriage and the baby who slept in the next room. When Todd and I were engaged we skimmed the chapter in the marriage books that said, "you don't just marry the man, you also marry his family." Perhaps this was true for some marriages, but not for ours. As if to prove our independence, we started out by moving to a new city. We thought it a good choice, a wise way to establish our new family. It was a full year before Todd's parents were able to visit our new home.

"Come upstairs for a few minutes," Amira said to me. "We'll go to the rooftop."

As Amira stood, Leila rubbed the lower part of her back, where the pain was. She would climb the stairs only after the baby was born, she told us.

"Go with Amira to the roof," Leila said. "It's too windy up there but we love the view from the top."

Amira left her straws and paper flowers scattered on Leila's coffee table and led me to the door, where we slipped on our shoes.

"The third floor is the best place to live, you know," Amira said, her voice amplified by the cement stairwell.

I laughed at Amira's joke because my own home was on the third floor of a family building. Living on the third floor gave me a buffer from the expectations—but only a slight one.

On the ground floor of my building lived a widow and her youngest son, not yet married. He was our landlord and it was his future home that we rented. Since the father's death this family had struggled. The wife of the eldest brother, living one floor below us, showed me how to hang laundry to dry on the rooftop, clipping the garments by hemlines to hide the inevitable rust spot from the wire laundry line. Our hot water heater had been broken when we moved in and weeks passed without the landlord making good on his promise to have it repaired. My downstairs neighbor had a functional hot water heater but never used it. "Too much for electricity," she said.

She encouraged me to save money on electricity by using my iron just once a week. I could not convince her that heating up an iron required very little power. But the confrontation over it all didn't come until weeks later.

The bill came to our landlord addressed in his dead father's name. Our first month there was in winter, and we kept our baby's room warm with an electric space heater, because it seemed safer than the propane heaters most people used. As a result the electric bill came in that month at twice the usual amount. We had the money and were glad to pay our young landlord the difference in cash. When he thanked us we had no idea that pressure was building.

We'd sought out a neighborhood on the opposite side of town from where Westerners usually rented. The adjustment would be harder for us, but we expected that our Arabic would be better for it, the bond to our Muslim friends stronger.

I loved our neighborhood. Goats roamed the streets eating vegetable peelings set out in plastic shopping bags by the housewives of the neighborhood in a simple and time-proven program of curbside recycling. The first time I put my own scraps out for the goats, I watched out the window until a goat, then two of them, nosed at my bag. The goats didn't care that a foreigner left the scraps. I was proud that I'd done this without anyone explaining it to me. It felt like the first step in belonging—to do the little things right without being told.

I wanted my one-year-old daughter to see the goats up close, so I carried Laurie down the stairs and out to the

street. The goats didn't look up from the cucumber peelings and apple cores. I lowered Laurie to let her stand, but
she clung to me. Then I felt a sting on the back of my leg;
I reached down to swat at it and felt another, and the next
rock hit my arm. The boys didn't run when I turned to face
them. I locked eyes with the tallest one. He smirked and
elbowed his comrade. Where were the mothers? If I knew
which boy belonged to which household I would tell their
mothers how their sons welcomed the foreigner. I took my
child back inside. The neighborhood boys threw stones at
me only the one time. But there were other ways to pester
the foreigner.

One little boy came to our front door to welcome us,
so I invited him in and served him juice and cookies. He
ate and drank and chatted to me in quick, low Arabic
that I couldn't follow. I was relieved when he left—but
then he visited every day and sometimes came twice in
a single afternoon. Perhaps I should have been thankful
for his company, but most days after a morning of Arabic
classes across town I was worn and culture shocked. On
my way home from class I held my tears only by watching the middle distance, looking past those who stared at
me. People stared as I stood waiting for the bus, stared
when I sat, stared when I rapped at the window to signal
the driver to stop. At home I could cry and no one would
see, no one would ask. It was a relief to close the door to
my apartment and be alone. I began to dread the sound
of children whooping their way home from school in the
late afternoon, because I knew that he would soon ring
the doorbell.

I stopped answering the door. He rang the bell every
fifteen minutes one afternoon until I answered, but he was
already gone, pounding down the stairs and out through

the front gate. Every day then he played ding-dong ditch with me—ring and run, ring and run. I decided to go to his mother for a solution. I patched together present-tense verbs in Arabic to explain, as best I could, what the child was doing. But I didn't really have proof. Before I confronted the mother I should catch the child in the act. I would have to get to the door more quickly when the bell sounded.

The next time the bell rang I grabbed a scarf to cover my head and I opened the door, ready to give chase.

Our landlord's mother stood there in plastic slippers, a light blanket wrapped around her shoulders against the cold. It took me a moment, but I thought to invite her in for tea. Instead of returning my smile she clicked her tongue, speaking swift and angry Arabic, so that I only caught a few words.

"Lights . . . all day . . . too much electricity."

Her hand reached around the doorway to sweep the inside wall until she found the switch and turned it off. The porch light had been on in broad daylight, and we must have left it burning since the last time we'd gone out in the evening two nights before. I hadn't even noticed. Why did it matter to her? We would pay every bill as we had the first, and I calculated that the extra electricity for one light bulb left burning would be only a few cents.

I apologized and she held up her fingers gathered at the tips as if holding a very small stone. I didn't understand this sign language, but her look was so intense that I nodded. With a last glance at the porch light my landlord's mother turned and went back down the stairs. As she descended her plastic sandals slapped hard against each step.

What did it matter if we used more electricity? It was our own business and not theirs. We thought like Americans, not Arabs. Their family name was on the electric bill.

Even when we paid in full, the money passed through their household—money spent on electricity that could have bought meat instead of cabbage. Our wastefulness reflected on them. Perhaps the dead father had never known a high electric bill.

I hung my husband's shirts and trousers like banners across our rooftop. I wanted to blend in and do things the ways that the women of my neighborhood did—but I couldn't. With modestly covered heads, the women hung their bras and panties in plain view. I suppose those intimate garments spoke of fertility . . . but I hung my private items to dry over a small rack in our bathtub. Tucked into our medicine cabinet were the pills I took to be sure my language studies weren't interrupted by the birth of another child.

The neighborhood watched to see how the foreigner, with his wife and child, would fit in. Eyes were also on our landlord's family, the ones who had taken us into their dwelling. The burden of letting an apartment to the outsiders must have been heavy.

The next time our landlord came to collect an electric bill he brought the man from across the street. Together they testified to how their wives kept electric usage low in their households. Todd sat with them and drank bitter coffee from a shared cup. Somehow our electricity had become a neighborhood concern—as if we were members of their tribe and our bill was paid with community money.

As evidenced by panties and bras on rooftop laundry lines, by aunts and cousins cheering the groom on the night of penetration, private business was not really private at all. We kept our underwear and our sex life to ourselves, and we wanted our electric bill to be confidential.

There was so much we didn't understand.

At the top of the stairwell, Amira opened the door to the rooftop and gestured for me to step out first. The breeze blew the wooden door shut behind us.

Full sun warmed the cement rooftop and its four-foot-high perimeter wall. Laundry lines crisscrossed overhead, attached to the reinforcement bars that extended vertically from the half wall. They looked almost like the monkey bars I climbed as a girl. As we passed the laundry Amira reached out and gave a feel to the blouses and socks hanging on the line. She batted at one of the socks so that it wrapped itself around the line like I always imagined my swing would wrap its chains around the top of the swing set if I could get enough momentum to go up and over the top.

As a child I practiced jumping from the swing while it was in full motion. Perhaps that daredevil jumping helped me to more easily make the leap away from my parents' home when I went to college and lived on my own, when I signed up for a research project in the Middle East. Did Amira even dream of such things? Or would the thought of separation be fearsome, like a free-fall into an abyss?

Below us the streets of our neighborhood snaked out of view past other family buildings in cement blocks rising out of the desert. On the roofs of many two- and three-story buildings laundry was hung out to dry, high above the dust of the street.

I picked out my own building not far away; on the roof my husband's shirts and my daughter's sleepers waved back to me. I wondered if our laundry would be dry when I got home.

My neighbors carried on the chore their mothers and sisters had done before them on rooftops across the city.

Amira's laundry hung on a line intersected by other lengths of line where Leila's clothes and her husband's and all the laundry of the extended family hung.

Amira pointed down to a stony park below us. A shepherd boy followed two scraggly sheep through the rocky area. The same boy often followed a mixed herd of sheep and goats through the field across from my own home. He cut his leg there once, and I brought him a clean rag to wrap the wound.

"It's a lovely park," I said to Amira.

"Ah, but it's not a park, O my friend."

Our neighborhood had at one time been on the outskirts of Amman, but new construction now defined the streets and lanes. Still, there were undeveloped areas waiting for growing families to build on them.

"An empty lot then," I said.

"I will tell you," Amira said. "It is the resting place of our fathers."

I still didn't understand. Amira put subtlety and poetics aside to speak in raw terms to the foreigner.

"For the dead."

The grounds finally resolved into a cemetery. Stones took shape as grave markers. We stood in silence, feeling the heat of the sun through our clothing, looking out over the neighborhood and the hills beyond. The shepherd boy picked up one of the sheep and lugged it out of the cemetery, dragging his stick against the headstones as he left.

If only Amira could have a child. Perhaps my next pregnancy would correspond with hers. We could go through it all together, with me learning the Arabic terms for morning sickness and cravings and that moment when abdominal flutterings become another person kicking to get out.

I was a little dizzy, whether from the height or from imagining the future. I turned from the view to watch my friend. Amira pulled her scarf to form a peak over her forehead, a visor against the sun's glare. She lifted her eyes to the hills. Her gaze stairstepped the mountain as if she were reading its history, as if her imagination climbed a ziggurat.

Far to our east lay the cradle of civilization, Mesopotamia, and Babylon with her hanging gardens. Further back up the great river of time lay Ur of the Chaldeans, where father Abraham took a wife before setting out across the desert.

Old Sarah was barren, too. Genesis tells us that she and father Abraham set up their tents across the desert by the oaks of Mamre. Sarah stayed in the tent when three strangers came along at the hottest part of the day to sit under the shade of the oaks with Abraham and share a drink of water.

Amira's bracelets caught the sun as she adjusted her headscarf. Surely Sarah wore gold as well, brought out from Abraham's wealth in Ur and Haran when God called him to leave and live in tents. Old Sarah's bracelets must have flashed in the sun when she pushed aside the tent flap to hear what the visitors said.

"Sarah will have a son."

For so many years, she'd carried the shame and shunted the pain by laughing at her infertility. And now—what were these men saying of an old woman well past menopause? She laughed.

Was it ancient Sarah's laughter echoing past the oaks of Mamre, across the desert and on through time?

But no. It was Amira who laughed. I laughed with her, for no reason at all except that the sun was low and warm and the graveyard was empty and the shepherd boy was strong.

When I got home late that afternoon it was time to start dinner. Laurie fussed and tugged at me as I mixed powdered milk in her sippy cup. I could already smell the onion and garlic from my neighbor's kitchen, but I was tired and not hungry after all the sugared tea at Leila's.

"I'm going up to the roof to take in the laundry before dark," I told my husband. "Will you watch Laurie a while longer?"

I climbed the two flights past the empty fourth-floor apartment to the rooftop where my laundry hung. I gave each garment a shake before folding it into the basket, and I stacked to one side the things that needed ironing.

Although the sunset view pulled at me I didn't let myself pause or look out past my rooftop until the last sock was off the line. After pushing the full basket over toward the stairwell door I leaned against the perimeter wall, chin on my arms, and looked out. The sun was gone, streets were empty, and smells of cooking wafted up from every side. When I came to the rooftop in midday a neighbor on an adjacent rooftop would wave or call a greeting to me. But in early evening the women of Amman cooked while their men waited for the meal.

Amira found her place entwined between the family name she was born with and the family name she married into and would give to her son. The families were important, their reputations and histories already well known by the community. The family line reached back generations through sons and fathers and grandfathers. Amira's part was to strengthen the unbroken cord by producing a son.

What did I know? My grandfather was an immigrant. He left Sweden in his teens to start a new life in the New

World, untethered. I had followed in his footsteps when I left America to come to the Middle East. Or had I? In a place where even the laundry lines testified to connection, to history, I felt alone.

When Amira looked at this landscape she saw the grandfathers and great-grandfathers who had settled the neighborhood and built up the desert from tents and flocks to become family buildings. She saw ghosts invisible to me. Amira saw her dead fathers and her unborn sons and the cord that bound her to them both.

The sun was gone and stars played in the half light near the moon. They hid when I looked directly at them, but if I focused my eyes on the horizon below I saw them in my peripheral vision, twinkling like Amira's eyes. The stars were there, and many more with them. As the night veiled us, stars would crowd the sky. Like a long memory, the promise returned to me. Something about stars too great to number and foreigners being grafted in.

From open windows below I heard clinking plates and voices and I knew that the landlord and his family were sitting down to eat. I also heard Todd's footsteps in the stairwell, and I took a last look at the twilit sky before turning to meet him.

"They've brought us a meal," he told me. "The landlord's mom knocked on the door just now and handed me a huge platter of rice and meat. It smells so good, and I'm starved."

After we ate we put Laurie to bed and turned out all the lights to save electricity. We sat by the window, watching the dark streets of our still and silent neighborhood. Above our rooftops, stars freckled the sky, promising good things on the way, a future and a hope, daughters and sons—more than we could ask or imagine.

CHAPTER 12

CITY OF REFUGE

The woman had no face. Skin stretched like putty across her bones in the earth tones of clay, becoming purplish below what had once been her ears. She was living evidence of chemical warfare—proof of the taxicab rumors that Saddam gassed his own people. *Don't believe everything you hear* I always reminded myself when I heard some dramatic tale or another. *Consider the source.* I could have reached out and touched her scars.

A garment like a large round tablecloth enveloped her, covering everything but her scarred face. Known in Iran as the chador, in Iraq this covering is called by its Arabic name, *abaya*. It was winter but she sat on a blanket spread over the frozen sidewalk and salted with a few coins. Her baby lay asleep on the blanket next to a half-empty milk bottle. Poverty was no excuse for letting a child lie on the cold ground in order to gain the pity of passersby. That's what I thought before I noticed her face.

Iraqi and American, we lived together in a city not our own. Amman's downtown is bordered by a Roman amphitheater on one side and the Corinthian columns of a Byzantine church on an adjacent hill. Amman belongs to her Arab children now, with reminders everywhere of other ancient cultures, ancient conquerors. She is a city of refuge for many. More than one-third of Jordan's citizens are Palestinian. The Iraqi population exploded after 1990. Some of Iraq's wealthiest citizens have become refugees. It used to be the Palestinians who were the poorest ones in Jordan—now it's the Iraqis.

Underneath the contracted skin, before the scars, had the Iraqi woman been pretty? Did her face burn before this baby was conceived, or after? Maybe this wasn't about Saddam at all, and there wasn't an evil man to blame for the burning. Every winter Jordanian newspapers carried reports of someone getting too close to a propane space heater on a cold day—or some housewife electrocuted when she forgot to unplug a washing machine before reaching in for the wet clothes. I refused to buy a propane heater the winter Todd and I moved to Amman with fifteen-month-old Laurie. Our electric space heater was less efficient than propane, so we bundled our toddler in sweaters and blankets that first year until we were able to move to the wealthy side of town—to a home with central heat. When we moved we also bought freedom from fear in the form of an expensive Italian washer with the proper grounding wires.

I came to the Middle East with a full portion of warnings and caution. The initial fears lost their power as life as a single woman in Damascus emboldened me. I was intrepid. I ran the gauntlet daily, crossing busy Damascus streets, stepping car width by car width across the road as vehicles zipped past me before and behind. I read Exodus in the mornings and Isak Dinesen in the evenings as the Call to

Prayer rang out over our Old City home in Damascus. In my journal I copied this passage from *Out of Africa*, on killing a pair of threatening lions:

> "And who is going to shoot them?" asked Nichols, "I am no coward, but I am a married man and I have no wish to risk my life unnecessarily." It was true that he was no coward; he was a plucky little man. "There would be no sense in it," he said. No, I said, I did not mean to make him shoot the lions.
>
> I then went in to find Denys. "Come now," I said to him, "and let us go and risk our lives unnecessarily. For if they have got any value at all, it is this: that they have got none."†

I was so struck by this passage that when I got back to the U.S. I read it out loud to a good friend. She gave me a look, that friend. Her look said I had it all wrong to think that my life had no value. I closed my journal. Who can argue with reason?

But that night when I was alone I wrote again in my journal that *I suspect there are times when the value of a life may not be only in the preservation of it.*

Todd was there in the Damascus study group with me. I wish I could say something romantic about how he watched me, wondering, waiting. But all that happened later, back in the States. Damascus itself was enough for us.

After we had been married just shy of two years, we spent all our savings to return to the Middle East the summer after Todd's first year of seminary. It was in that romantic summer, crossing a downtown street in Damascus, that the blur of adventure around us stopped for a

---

† Isak Dinesen, *Out of Africa* (New York: Random House, 1938), 232–233.

moment. My pace was off and a passing car skimmed my left hand, bruising my knuckles and scraping the skin off the middle one. I felt for the first time my own mortality, the delicacy of life and marriage and future.

I stared at the Iraqi woman on the ground. Did the cold wind make her scars hurt, or could she even feel the cold through damaged nerve ends? I've read that burn victims live in constant pain forever after. What if this had happened to me? Because it hadn't, I could go on blithely saying that God was good. But what did this lady think of the God who melts faces?

My friend Ben was downtown that day, drinking tea just one storefront away from where I stood watching the Iraqi woman. Ben leaned against the counter of a tea stand, dressed like a modern Arab in trousers and dress shoes, shirt tucked in and buttoned over a modest undershirt—but above the collar he was still a pale, blond, round-faced American college kid. While I was watching the Iraqi woman and her baby, Ben was watching me.

I knew Ben from Oregon. "Ben has a great heart," I would say to my college friends, as if he were my younger brother. I had a sisterly affection for Ben and patience for the way he was slow to speak and clumsy with his words when he did. I watched out for him back in those days, but as it goes with kid brothers, so it went with Ben. He arrived in Jordan a semester ahead of Todd and me. He studied Arabic at the same school we would attend. When we arrived, Ben was waiting to help us settle in. We set up house. Started Arabic studies. Ben was in the class across the hall, and I would see him at breaks. I'd known Ben long before I ever heard Todd's name. He was a solid reminder of my life in Oregon, of who I was back when I spoke a language fluently and glided through life gracefully and made friends with ease.

As adventure in Amman gave way to culture shock Ben turned up here and there in arched doorways and on crowded downtown streets. A face from my old home. At times I felt that the entire world, past and present, was all right there in Amman with me in one form or another, in architecture and ethnicity, in ruins and in flesh.

Running into Ben off campus a few years earlier might have meant grabbing some coffee together at The Beanery or sitting down on the grass to chat if it was a warm day. But here? It wouldn't be proper, and there was no place for us to go in this culture of men's tea shops and women's curtained salons.

"Come on," Ben said to me, "I have something to show you."

I followed him away from the tea stand and around the corner. He stopped in front of a store overflowing with all sorts of brass items; huge decorative trays and plaques leaned up against the storefront windows. Ben held the door open and I went in ahead of him. The shop owner knew Ben and spoke a clear Jordanian dialect that was easy to follow.

"Ahh, she is your sister?"

Now I understood why I could come here with an unmarried man and not put my honor at stake.

The shop owner knew what Ben wanted to see, and he moved a stack of trays to reveal piles of canvas underneath. They were paintings, scenes from a traditional town with robed figures walking under arched labyrinths through an ancient city. I knew these streets, these people. Here in oil paint was my life in Damascus, before I feared cars or washing machines or evil men in high places. Through one open door in these Arabic city scenes I could make out a fountain, an inner garden. A place to rest.

These paintings piled oil-to-fabric over stacks of brass trays were the work of Iraqi artists who fled Baghdad at the end of 1990. Each painting grabbed a moment and froze it in oil, telling stories about life in Baghdad before the exile—when life was good. When God was good.

I picked one up and flicked at the dust chunks clinging to the bottom edge. Most of the artwork I saw that day was in bright colors—red and cobalt and green, the vignettes filling the interior of the field but fading toward the edges so there was a wide band of canvas, primed but colorless, framing each scene. This one that I picked up was different, all in the terra cotta and purple shades of a sunset at Petra, scene and color extending nearly to the edge of the canvas. The extra brush strokes gave it a sense of wholeness, as if this painting were complete in a way the others weren't.

The paint stood out from the canvas, thick and dimensional. It looked like some of the oils had been laid on with a knife instead of a brush, smooth to the point where the knife lifted from the canvas, and on those edges there was a ridge, a scar.

After Ben and I left the shop I went straight to a framer's studio and selected a frame with brass detailing—my own tip of the hat to the brass shop owner who helped some Iraqi artist. This scene has kept me company in four different homes, in two countries. Exotic, ancient, it is part of our North American household now. Sometimes I stand in front of it—trying to get back, just for a moment, to remember the scent of cardamom-spiced coffee and the sound of Arabic music swirling through those Old City corridors and peaceful garden courtyards. If anyone walks in the room I quickly move to finish folding laundry.

Most of the figures in this painting are walking away, scarves thrown over shoulders, robes swaying. But one figure in the foreground faces me, my piles of laundry, my life. A woman, featureless, with just a scrape of clay-colored paint where she should have a face.

CHAPTER 13

EVIL EYE

The curse of the evil eye could dry up my friend Hala's breast milk or make her twin babies desperately ill, sucking the life right out of them with a strong bout of diarrhea and dehydration. In the desert, moisture is blessing and life. Dryness is death.

Jars full of dried roots and seeds and spices lined the shop's shelves from floor to ceiling. An old woman leaned in and whispered to the proprietor; he took down a jar stuffed with sprigs of the vital herb. For two babies she would need double, so the proprietor counted out herbs first, then coins. She walked home through the bazaar hunching her back to protect the delicate packet she carried under her coat. Once home, she dropped her coat and scarf on the sideboard and closed the kitchen door behind her.

After wiping out the sink so it was good and dry she laid the herbal portion in a bunch next to the drain. The old woman struck a match and held it against the dried herbs. They began to crackle and burned quickly, flames low in the sink to prevent fire from catching hold of anything else in the house. As the pieces burned, five pops made her jump then nod and smile: five jealous looks of the evil eye broken in advance. After the herb burned itself out, the charm now firm and good, she scraped the ashes into a fabric pouch.

When I arrived, Hala's mother-in-law sat on the floor mat next to the swaddled babies. She narrowed her eyes when she looked at me; she shifted to position herself on the front edge of the mat so that her grandson was out of my sight. I saw only his blanket and the blue beads safety-pinned to it. His twin sister had a matching set of beads. The beads protect from the evil eye and the accidental curse that might sap health and moisture and life.

Hala came into the room to greet me, her hair still wet from the bath I'd interrupted. If water signifies blessing and life then hot water is the superlative sign of blessing. I lived without a hot water heater.

Our young landlord kept promising to fix it. "Tomorrow, if Allah wills," he would pledge, one hand over his heart. Days into weeks I heated water on the stovetop to fill a wide bucket for Laurie's bath. Todd and I showered in jolting cold bursts from the rooftop water tank.

Hala glowed from her bath and when I greeted her with a kiss, first on the right cheek then the left, her face warmed my own cold and dry skin.

The boy cried out in that rusty bellow of a newborn. Hala sat cross-legged on the thick floor mat that served as a low sofa, Bedouin-style, across one side of the room. She took the baby on her lap. Her mother-in-law, now relieved of guarding the twins from the evil eye of the foreigner, left the room. Hala patted the mat beside her with one hand and with the other she pulled her dress open to nurse. I sat cross-legged and admired the sleeping baby girl on the mat between us. Seeing a bit of dirt on her forehead, I reached to gently rub it off.

"Don't touch it—no! It's just a little ash, very clean. For the evil eye."

Hala leaned to show me that her nursing son wore a matching smear of ash. He was asleep again after just a few sucks, and Hala closed the front of her dress with one hand, drawing out her necklace before doing up the top button. On the long chain a gold pendant rested just over her breast: a stylized hand. The fingers were filled in with filigree curlicues, and from the center of the palm stared a blue eye. It was a Hand of Fatima, named after the prophet Mohammed's daughter. The eye in the palm protected the wearer—an eye to ward off an eye.

"The old people believe in it," Hala shrugged. "We have to be careful."

The old women of Arabia tell the story of a baby boy with skin like alabaster and a cry as sweet as music, born ten years ago, or twenty, or five hundred. His mother was too careless. She dressed him in fine clothes and brought him out into the main square. There she saw one of her friends from school days, who was married but had no children. The schoolmate proclaimed the baby the loveliest, most perfect child under the sun.

That very hour the baby became sick. He had diarrhea and he vomited again and again until all the milk had gone from him and what he vomited came yellow and vile like the urine of a camel. The life went out of him. He became so dry that when his skin was touched it remained in peaks, like dunes in the desert.

The schoolmate didn't intend to cast the evil eye. She truly admired the baby, even loved him. She couldn't help it. Every woman wants a son. The schoolmate envied without realizing; she longed for him, and the spell was cast.

Before living in the Middle East, I thought of the evil eye as a dirty look—a conscious wish of evil. But the power is unintentional. The curse is enacted by simple envy. The one who casts the curse is a victim too, nearly always unaware of the danger, like a carrier of a dangerous virus—not susceptible for some reason, certainly not wanting to pass on the deadly curse, but unable to prevent it.

If when I held Hala's son I had yearned for a son of my own, a son with the same swirl of hair and tiny ears, the spell would be cast. That evening Hala might notice that the baby's tongue seemed dry and that he didn't nurse for as long as he should. But she wouldn't know for sure, even then.

The fact that I'd noticed the ashes and the blue beads demonstrated that the talismans worked. They caught my attention and distracted me. They would work the same way for any visitor, for any stranger who might envy the babies or Hala's happiness with them. The evil eye's first jealous glance is the most potent. The wearer is protected from that piercing curse only when the look is caught and diffused by a spot of ash or amulet of blue.

My friend snugged the blanket tighter about her son and positioned the blue-beaded safety pin to hold the wrap before laying him back down next to his twin sister. Already the baby girl stirred and grimaced. Hala sighed, screwing up her own face in imitation of her daughter's.

"Oh, but these babies cry all night."

Hala lifted her bundled daughter and stood. She walked back and forth across the room and jounced to quiet the baby. Under Hala's bare feet oriental rugs spread from wall to wall all in the same design, laid out in alternating directions like an Escher drawing, each one fitting against the next so that not one inch of the tile floor was exposed. I wondered which I would prefer, given a choice—the sleep-starved weariness of a new mother resting in a warm and comfortable home, or uninterrupted sleep someplace empty and cold.

My own apartment had no carpets and little furniture. The cement and tile construction held winter's chill. Everyone said we'd appreciate the cool tile come summer. We returned home from language school each day to our unheated home and a broken hot water tank and kept our coats on even indoors. It was an easy walk down the hill to where Hala lived. I would slip my heels out of my shoes even before her door opened, ready to step from the cold onto warm, soft carpets.

Of course I was jealous of Hala—in a way. She'd married into a wealthy family and had no worries about hot water heaters or carpets or furniture. Her husband, Mansour, worked at his father's furniture store, up the hill past our apartment. We'd met him our first week in Jordan when we bought two plastic chairs and a small table and he insisted on delivering them himself. Mansour tried to sell us a dresser and a bed frame, but we were using empty boxes placed on their sides for open cardboard shelves. In these we stacked our clothes. Without a bed frame, our sleeping mats could be leaned up against the wall during the day, allowing floor space for Laurie to play. The apartment had only one bedroom and we thought we'd put off buying more furniture just in case we found someplace bigger in a few months. I had no good reason to envy Hala. We'd made our choices.

Carrying a serving tray, Hala's mother-in-law came back into the room. She set down the tray and poured out a milky beverage full of crushed nuts and sweetened with coconut. This drink was to celebrate the births and also to help Hala's uterus shrink and her milk come in. It was tasty and made me think of my own days at home after my daughter's birth, before we left the U.S. When my newborn didn't gain weight and I worried that my breast milk wasn't enough for her, my midwife told me to drink beer. I dislike the taste of beer so I shrugged it off as an old wives' tale and drank more water. But this sweet concoction was something I could have enjoyed as a new mother—if someone had been around to make it for me. I drained my cup, expecting to have a second serving pressed upon me, in Arab style. Hala's mother-in-law poured a refill only for the new mother before she carried the tray, with my empty cup on it, out of the room. It's not like an Arab hostess to leave her guest thirsty and dry.

Beware, you mothers. Smudge the ashes just so on your son's head. If someone praises your baby too much, diffuse the curse by saying, "Oh, but he is so dirty now." Spit on the child to apply moisture and prevent the drying curse. Better to soil the child's face while he is living than to bury him under dry sand when he has died.

Pin blue beads to his blanket and keep him at home for forty days after the birth, away from the eyes of the envious ones. If a woman, even your own sister, should look upon the child for too long, you must break her gaze or your child will absorb the drying curse. If a blue bead shatters you will know it has succeeded in deflecting the evil eye.

Those foreigners with blue eyes—they draw near with kindness and will praise your baby. They come to our land and our homes with envy. Beware, you mothers.

Of course Hala suspected me. Our friendship seemed a deep one after only a few months . . . but for generations the superstition had been passed from mother to daughter through lines of blood. In retrospect it seems obvious which would win out.

When Lawrence of Arabia roamed these sands an old Bedouin woman told him that his blue eyes were the color of death. They were like the sky seen through the eye sockets of a bleached skull, she said, keeping her distance.

I was the foreigner—my eyes a fair match for those blue beads. And Hala had something I didn't—that blessing every Arab couple prays for. She had a son.

Hala sat with the girl and nursed her. The baby ate with slurps and snorts and Hala watched the child from under heavy eyelids, lifting her gaze with a start every few moments to glance at the other twin or at me. She looked so weary, and I could feel again those early weeks of my own motherhood: thirsty for sleep, waking in dread that my newborn would cry out and I'd have to get up—then a worse fear driving me out of bed to be sure that my silent baby was breathing. I wondered if Hala felt a chill in her stomach thinking of the evil eye as I did thinking of SIDS. Does a baby outgrow the threat of the curse as it outgrows the danger of crib death? A new baby is a blessing from God. But, admiring Hala's double blessing, I felt more relief than jealousy.

"You must stay for a meal," Hala said. "Mansour will go and bring your husband. You can celebrate with us for our son's health."

And for your daughter's, I thought.

The day when we first met Mansour at the furniture shop he had loaded the furniture into the back of his truck and crowded Todd, Laurie, and myself into the cab along with him in order to deliver it.

"My wife is an English teacher," he said. "She will want to meet you."

Hala was still teaching half time when I met her but the early contractions started a few weeks later—just about the time my Arabic classes started—and she was placed on bed rest. Hala wasn't able to venture out with me as I learned to bargain with merchants in Arabic and catch the right bus from our neighborhood to go downtown. During those last long weeks of her pregnancy she became a silent partner—a big sister always eager to hear my stories and offer advice. Hala warned me to keep my eye on the man at the produce stand, the big guy with the fat fingers.

He weighed my selection of vegetables on a balancing scale, my cucumbers on one side and his measured weights on the other. His thumb pressed down on the cucumber side of the scale, adding weight to my purchase. The realization shot through me. He was trying to cheat me just as Hala had warned. Even before I spoke, I thought of how pleased Hala would be that I had applied her lessons so well. When I confronted the big produce guy in my clumsy Arabic, he lifted his hands from the scale and added two small cucumbers to bring it into balance, like a pair of fat green thumbs. He bagged the cucumbers and grabbed a long, curved knife from somewhere. With it he sawed a cluster of four-inch-long bananas from the large bunch hanging on a rope at the front of the stand. He handed the bananas to me along with the cucumbers and wouldn't let me pay.

I brought the bananas to Hala and she laughed and kissed my cheek and found some chocolates so we could celebrate. In those days before the babies were born Hala had been so interested in my progress in Arabic, my adjustment to the Middle East. She helped me study for tests and she delighted in every account I gave of a foreigner's life out on the Jordanian streets. Hala was interested in hearing about my life in America, too. I didn't see that things were changing. Interest and concern were morphing into envy.

"Your hair is so smooth, so soft," she would say to me. By contrast, Hala's hair was coarse and strained at the clip she used to fasten it at the back of her head. I mentioned to Hala that American beauticians use chemicals to relax kinks and make hair like hers straight. Hala asked me if my own hair had been curly once and if I used the beautician's chemicals. Why weren't such products available in Arab salons? If she gave me money, couldn't I have someone from America ship the right chemicals to Hala in Jordan? Her blast of questions seemed out of character at the time, but I thought it was only the end of pregnancy making her short-tempered. There were days when I kept my scarf on even inside Hala's house.

Hala's interest in America wasn't cultural. She probed for what she might be able to get through me. We thought we were escaping materialism when we moved to the Middle East, where culture is reputed to be all about community, hospitality, and relationship. Sometimes my Arab friends asked if I could help them get papers to travel to the U.S., to study or to find a job. But not Hala. She just wanted to lead a comfortable life there in Amman. I don't think she believed me when I told her I had no special contacts in America, that my friends there couldn't afford to export things via airmail.

Once the twins were born, Hala couldn't watch over me as she had those first weeks. Her life was full with motherhood, and even when I told her about Arabic class or the argument I'd had with the landlord's mother, Hala's eyes closed. She sometimes drifted off as we sat together. I suppose I had done the same when my own newborn kept me awake nights. Even as Hala's mother-in-law set out the dinner things with a pitcher of water and extra glasses for Todd and me, I knew that our visit should be short. We would say goodnight right after the meal, go on home to our chilled apartment, and leave Hala and Mansour to tend their newborn babies away from the eyes of foreigners.

The drying curse manifests in many ways, just as the summer winds blow the many sands to and fro in different directions until the traveler knows not earth from sky or his right hand from his left. A man lost in the desert will perish slowly as life is sucked from him by sand and sun. And so the cursed one will likewise whither.

Great thirst is one sign. The skin may shrivel or peel. Even the heart may become parched so that it devours all hope and good will.

Even in my own worldview jealousy is a curse of sorts. The result of jealousy is always something drying up, whether trust or friendship. But I speak figuratively and Arabs look for tangible evidence of the curse—a family well going dry or a mysterious illness dehydrating a child until her skin is dry like an old woman's and life drains away.

The cloth was spread on the floor and dishes already set around when Mansour arrived with Todd and Laurie. The men removed their shoes at the door and stepped onto the carpet. Todd set the portable high chair down inside the door and squatted to unlace Laurie's shoes. She was bouncy and eager to come in; she loved this home with soft, warm floors to crawl on and real furniture to lean up against.

We sat on the floor to eat, first soup and fried potatoes, then roasted kebab and vegetables and rice. Our portable high chair was designed to strap to an adult chair, like a booster seat with a tray attached—but we set it directly on the floor so that Laurie ate at our level, keeping her mess on the tray with no danger of her crawling into the platter of meat and rice.

"It's a wonderful seat for a baby," Hala said. "So perfect for an Arabic meal."

My mouth was dry. I reached for the pitcher and refilled my cup.

"Did you buy the seat here in Jordan? Was the price very high?"

The water didn't help. My mouth still felt dry.

"We would love to have such a thing for our babies."

Before Hala could ask me whether my friends in America could send one I excused myself and retreated to the bathroom.

Hala envied me my freedom as much as anything. I crossed borders and could buy and bring with me what I wanted. She was bound to one place, one culture, one set of goods and technology and superstitions. When Hala looked at me she peered at my world as through a telescope turned backward. She saw only the sparkle of the brightest things, and she wanted them to come near. If I had offered her my child's high chair, a gift, she would have taken it and looked for a way to trade my hair for hers as well. That's what I felt about my friend Hala as I locked myself in her bathroom for my self-imposed time out.

The hot-water heater was across from the toilet. Its pilot light shone blue through a small glass window like yet another eye guarding against the foreigner's jealousy. And I was jealous. We'd been living weeks and weeks without hot water. I longed to fill the tub with water so hot it would shock my skin and leave my submerged parts as red as if I'd been slapped. My skin was thirsty for the water that would make my blood circulate and warm me for hours, even after the water drained away.

Running water in the sink, I let it warm my hands, my wrists; I leaned in so the water flowed almost to my elbows. The towel I used to dry my hands was rough from a wash with no fabric softener, hung out on a rooftop line to dry.

I returned to the supper spread on the floor. Hala used her own spoon to feed Laurie. My friend blew and tested the broth carefully before bringing it to my child's mouth, just as I would do.

"She is so clever, so happy," Hala said as she helped Laurie drink water from a glass, catching the drips with a tissue before they fell. "She never cries."

I reminded Hala that her own babies would grow to be toddlers, that over time they would cry less and sleep more. She seemed not to hear me as she spooned more rice, carefully cooled, into my child's mouth. I felt a crick in my neck from sitting on the floor with nothing to lean against.

At the side of the room the twins slept with their ashen foreheads, blue beads, and full tummies. There was no drying out, no illness, no evidence of the curse upon this household.

Laurie squirmed in the seat and pushed Hala's spoon away. I clicked the tray off and lifted her out, again excusing myself from the table. Laurie snuggled into my arms and lay her head on my shoulder. As I rubbed her back to help her drift off to sleep, I felt her cheek against mine. Our first winter in Jordan left her skin rough and dry.

In stones of turquoise we see the eyes of the desert sky, under which our ancestors migrated these sands with flocks and herds. Those ancient Bedouin tribes welcomed the wanderer to eat and sleep in their tents—but with precaution. Our fathers mounted turquoises at the entrance to their tents to protect all who dwelled therein from the curse. Just as water does not absorb the image of a tree but reflects it, so blue stones bounce the power of the evil eye away from the tent. When a stone deflects the curse the stone will crack or break. When you hear it pop you will know that you have been delivered from the curse. But

beware. Once deflected, the curse has not been abolished. Do not relax yourself. Remain diligent and watchful.

When our fathers ceased their wandering and settled near the waters to cultivate olive trees they hung the blue stones on the branches. Who knows what covetous neighbor might look upon the orchard for too long? A man must tend his flocks, his trees. He must weed and water and pluck the fruit in due season. By the time the leaves wither it is too late. Then, though he water his trees with tears, the curse will destroy them. The wise man knows that he must protect his property from the drying curse. If this is true for flocks and lands, how much more precious is the home?

The turquoise is a repellent talisman. You shall bind it to your infant's wrist and on his garment. Hang the talismans on your doorposts of your house and on your gates. Take care lest moisture and life be siphoned from you.

Ramadan came, our Arabic studies intensified, and we didn't visit Hala and Mansour as often as we had before the twins were born. We broke the fast with them one evening at sunset, and they told us what a blessing it was for Ramadan to fall during the cool of winter rather than the heat of summer. It was much harder to fast when the days were hot and long, and water forbidden.

Perhaps it was our move to Jordan that made Ramadan weather so pleasant, Mansour said. I wasn't sure how to react to such a senseless statement. We brought blessing with us from America for all Jordanians, he said, and especially for Hala and the twins.

Perhaps the blessing, like the hot water, flowed only to Hala and Mansour.

When Todd asked why our landlord would make empty promises to us about fixing the water tank, Mansour changed the subject. My Arab sister and her husband were no longer our cultural counselors. I should have seen it then. The friendship was drying out.

Ramadan was nearly over, Mansour said. He made us promise to come back for the three-day celebration at the end of the month. Since the end of Ramadan is determined by the reappearance of the moon we didn't know ahead of time exactly what day it would arrive.

We woke one morning to find the celebration unleashed. Neighbors were out in fancy clothes, children sucking on candy, sipping drinks right there where all could see, walking, everyone strolling and smiling and calling greetings across the road to friends and strangers. I dressed Laurie in the new outfit and white shoes her grandmother had sent from America, and we went to do our visiting.

In the three days that follow Ramadan friends and family visit back and forth, eating special date cookies and generally feasting and celebrating friendship as well as the end of the fast. We visited the neighbors in our building and across the road, and then we walked down the hill to Mansour and Hala's house. Our daughter walked between us, holding our hands and swinging forward every few steps. No one stared at us that day. It was as if we were no longer the foreigners and there was no more division between blue eyes and brown. We were part of the community—just like any other family in our neighborhood, dressed up, walking and laughing, celebrating the end of Ramadan all together.

I got ready to slip my shoes off while Todd knocked at Mansour and Hala's door. The metal knocker was in the shape of a hand, knuckles flexed and facing out, so any blue eye in the palm was hidden. It made sense to use a Hand of Fatima as a doorknocker, I thought. The front door is like the eye of the home—through it all things enter, whether evil or blessing. But this Hand of Fatima was not a flat hand of protection. It was a fist.

There was no answer. They must be out visiting neighbors, Todd said. We'd have to come back in a couple of hours and try again. We turned from the door and went back up the hill. Laurie fussed and refused to walk. Todd picked her up and I took off her shoes and socks, brushing the bottoms of her feet to sweep away any small stones or sand. Between her toes were small cracks with dry skin peeling away. Once the stores opened up after the celebration I'd buy antifungal ointment at the pharmacy. Her feet had been warm in socks and shoes all winter, but I hadn't really thought about keeping them dry. Moisture is not always a blessing.

Even as spring warmed the tile floors and we left windows open to let in the sunshine, we knew that we needed to move. The landlord no longer made promises about fixing the water tank and he began asking Todd when our Arabic studies would be finished, where we would go next.

Then the cursed *khamseeny* came, those dry winds that blow the desert right into the house through every crack. The winds last nearly two months, on and off. That first day of khamseeny I was thankful for the breeze, not realizing that it carried dust through the windows, soiling my floors, my furniture, even my clothes in those open cardboard shelves. I had to search through boxes to find the hand lotion, because even when I closed the windows to shut out the khamseeny my skin itched with dryness.

Across town we found a new place to live with two bedrooms and central heat. One day after our Arabic classes we hired a pickup truck driver who helped Todd load our sleeping mats and plastic chairs and boxes of books and clothes into the back of the truck. What we owned made up one perfect truckload. Todd locked the apartment door and handed the key to our landlord. Then he squeezed into the cab of the pickup with a box of books crammed between himself and the driver. Hanging from the rearview mirror was a disc; in its center, a blue eye. I crossed the street to wait for the bus, since there had been no room in the pickup for my daughter and me.

Todd and I had thought the move would take two pickup loads; we planned to walk down and say goodbye to Mansour and Hala in between trips. The bus pulled up and I hesitated—it would only take a few minutes to go on down the hill to their place. The new apartment across town had a working hot water tank and a bathtub with brown and pink and orange tiles. That night I would have my first hot bath in months.

I got on the bus.

I sat next to an open window, my daughter on my lap. As the bus pulled itself up the hill and out of our first neighborhood, the khamseeny winds started up again, blowing dust into the bus—passengers jumped to push the windows up tight and closed. I promised myself that I would come back to the neighborhood and visit Hala once we'd settled into the new home. But my intention dried up and blew away. In the three and a half years we lived in Amman, I didn't return to our old neighborhood after that day. I never saw Hala again.

Long ago a stranger came to us from beyond the desert, from that distant edge where blue meets blue. Like a shivering child, she crept into our tent for shelter. We warmed and filled her, with due precaution for jealousy's curse. She learned well, and we rejoiced when she took her first steps. She became one of us, if only for a season.

She came from a dark and sodden land where green-dripping trees grow suffocatingly high and close. Her blue eyes stared without seeing into the aching beauty of our wide bright sky framed in by sand beneath and light above. Who knows what she saw there? What she found here to envy?

The season of her sojourn passed, and she crept away as quietly as she had come. We did not weep, and neither were we surprised. From the beginning we knew she would leave us. Now we tell her story to our children.

Outside the bus, airborne sand and dirt made the sun's light dim and nearly orange, as if a thousand and one fires burned in the city. The sky was so dusty that when I turned to look out the back window the neighborhood behind me disappeared into the haze. The bone-dry fog surrounded and obscured Hala's home so that she was beyond where my eyes could reach, swallowed up by the shifting walls of the parched desert.

CHAPTER 14

FROM THE BALCONY

Our new home was a pie-shaped apartment on the second floor of a three-story building close to the language school. It had a working hot water tank. A narrow balcony wrapped around the pie-crust perimeter of our apartment. We kept Laurie's Tyke Bike on the rooftop, where she could ride as I hung out the laundry. Sometimes I lifted her up to see over the parapet out across the rooftops of the city that had become our home.

Directly below us in the wedge-shaped building, on street level, a cranky old man ran a tiny shop no bigger than a concession booth. He sold cigarettes and candy and an odd assortment of soaps and detergents. He frowned at us as we came and went. When we left for language school each morning he scolded us for clanking the front door shut. When we came home each afternoon he pinched one eye shut and glared at us through the other. In the evening, after he'd closed up shop, we laid a small bag of the day's rubbish at the curb, as did all our neighbors.

Starting before dawn garbage collectors in bright orange jumpsuits patrolled the neighborhood on foot, collecting sacks of rubbish in wheelbarrows and carrying them to the nearest communal dumpster. The cranky shop owner scolded us for placing trash too near his shop entrance. We learned to carry our sack catty-corner across the street and plop it on top of the neighbor's trash pile. I bought laundry soap from the cranky shopkeeper, to try and make peace with him, but the brands he sold were as cheap in quality as they were in price. The detergent left white powdery streaks on our clean wash.

Our street twisted down the hill toward the Abdali bus station where I heard that first Call to Prayer and saw two Muslim men praying early morning prayers. Halfway down, my friend Reema lived with her husband and a son, Yezzin, who was Laurie's age and attended the same pre-school. I first met Reema on the street, when she recognized Laurie—one of several foreign children at Yezzin's preschool. Reema greeted me in Arabic, and we conversed for several minutes. Then she asked a question I couldn't understand. After a few attempts, she surprised me by switching to English.

"I'm saying that Yezzin and Laurie are sweethearts," Reema said.

"You speak English?"

"Of course. But not as well as you speak Arabic."

I appreciated the obvious false flattery. Reema's English was perfect. We traded off meeting for play dates at her house and mine. Reema showed me how to clean a messy toddler—face or bottom first, depending—by holding her up to the sink with the offending part held near the running water. The free hand is cupped to splash water and rinse. No need for expensive baby wipes or even washrags. I kept all my children clean with this no-rag method, long after Reema left Amman and emigrated to Canada with her husband and Yezzin.

Yezzin was a wild child and Reema had no control over him. When she and Yezzin came to our apartment one fall day, Reema and I became caught up in a discussion of Islamic history and didn't notice right away when the apartment became far too quiet.

"Where are the children?" I asked.

"Oh—the balcony!" Reema exclaimed, her fears the same as mine.

Sure enough, the children were out on the balcony, standing on plastic chairs and leaning out over the street. Between them on the ledge was a bucket of alphabet letter magnets, which one by one they released over the edge into the street below. Reema yanked Yezzin off the chair and swatted his bottom. I grabbed Laurie in one hand and the bucket of ABCs in the other, setting both down on the balcony floor. In the street below me the old man from the candy and cigarette booth hobbled around in the street picking up a bright red J, green L, blue plastic M. He wore a long gray kaftan with a man's suit jacket over it. He didn't look up as he bent to retrieve the bright plastic ABCs. I was horrified. If only I could ignore the whole situation and pretend I knew nothing about it. But the ABC evidence obviously incriminated the one English-speaking child in the building. I wonder how you say 'fess up in Arabic? I left the children with Reema while I went down to apologize and collect the alphabet letters. He didn't lecture this time. Just placed the magnetic letters in a small plastic bag as if I'd bought them from his booth. I felt so chagrined that I selected two bars of soap to purchase from him. I dashed upstairs to find some money and stash the alphabet evidence—then back down again to pay for the soap. He placed my small purchase in another bag and gave me my change. The soap held such a strong perfume that it made me sneeze. After a few days I concealed it deep in a sack of trash and took the bundle all the way to the dumpster down the hill near Reema's home, lest our cranky neighbor sniff me out.

In our photo albums from Jordan years, Yezzin chases Laurie through the pages, now taking turns sitting on a plastic chair, now dashing out to the balcony. When she looks through the pictures Laurie will chuckle and say "that naughty Yezzin—he was my best friend." But Laurie doesn't really remember Yezzin. She was two years old when his family emigrated to Canada. I remember for her, with snapshots and with stories.

We finished our Arabic studies and Todd found work, so our student visas were changed to residency cards. We moved to a large, ground-floor apartment on the far west side of Amman. Our home had a lovely covered patio off the kitchen and grape arbor out back, next to the laundry line. No more lugging wet clothes up flights of stairs. Plenty of room for Laurie to play. By that time I was pregnant with our second child.

Ashley was born early in September. Her birth certificate is written in swooping Arabic script, as is the booklet containing her immunization records. Ashley was an easy baby, sleeping through the night for the first time when she was just ten days old. Laurie showed no jealousy for the baby. She begged me to bring Ashley's bouncy seat into the playroom, "So she can watch me play, Mama." Todd worked from his study in the front of the house. For the first time since we'd come to Jordan we had a phone line and Internet connection. We picked up our mail at the neighborhood post office two blocks away. A teacher at the preschool around the corner knocked at the door to ask if I would teach English for them. No more preschool for my babies, I decided. No more work or studies for me. For the first time since we arrived in Jordan I would be a stay-at-home mom. My heart was full with home and family. Life was so good.

CHAPTER 15

EXILES

You will leave everything you love most:
this is the arrow that the bow of exile
shoots first. You will know how salty
another's bread tastes and how hard it
is to ascend and descend
another's stairs.

Paradiso XVII: 55–60
Dante, *The Divine Comedy*

A night storm thrashes at the rooftop. Streaks of light descend followed by booms of thunder—or perhaps cannons or bombs. The heavens roar; the deluge is unleashed. Man and woman are driven out. They dash to find shelter beneath canyon or tree, glancing back to their ruined home. There is no time to mourn, to say goodbye. The strong grab and go while the weak are left to receive the enemy soldiers or the hurricane's flood. It is an old story, the motif played out again and again through history. Flaming swords guard the closed door. There is no return for the exiles.

Mrs. Jalal handed me a small drawstring pouch sewn of soft fabric, imprinted with the name of a local jeweler.

"For the baby," she said.

I opened the pouch and pulled out a pendant of the Virgin, 18-carat gold with navy enamel forming her robe and scarf. We're Protestants but few of our Muslim friends understood the difference between Catholic and Protestant. Had I been a Muslim the pendant would have been a Hand of Fatima or Koranic verses or Allah's ninety-nine names written on two sides of the charm in microscopic script.

Dr. Jalal, our landlord, pronounced newborn Ashley "perfect" and Mrs. Jalal made an Arabic-English word play when she told me to use her first name, Tamam. We all laughed. Tamam is the Arabic word for perfection.

As I cut slices of cake Todd told the latest news from the U.S.—that his father would recover slowly from the minor stroke, but he should gain back all his abilities. Todd's brother Jeff was on his way to Nebraska. "I don't know why, but I feel scared," Jeff had said.

Dr. and Mrs. Jalal, a Palestinian pediatrician and his jet-setting wife, lived on the floor above us. They rented out their first and third floors to foreigners. Our home on the first floor was the most private in the building, with a separate entrance that didn't connect to the stairwell leading to the upper floors.

It's ironic how many words we spent explaining my father-in-law's future after the stroke. First week he'll be moved home, we said as if prophesying. A month later he'll start going in to work for half days. In a year he'll hardly know he had the stroke . . .

We stood on the porch after saying goodnight to the Jalals. Under the streetlight, the green leaves on the olive trees appeared a lifeless gray.

Todd turned to me. "I love you, Babe." He kissed me, and then we went inside to put our daughters to bed. I fell asleep, thankful and content.

The phone rang and rang in my dream, but when I tried to run down the hall my legs were too heavy, weighed down by sleep and by the winter quilt.

I woke, with my heart beating fast, to see Todd's form sitting on the edge of the bed in the dark.

"Todd? Did the phone ring?"

"It has to be about Dad. They'll call again."

I got up and checked on the girls. Reaching out to touch the baby's back, I felt the rise and fall of her breathing. Todd put on the living room light, and I unfolded a receiving blanket to wear over my shoulders like a shawl. I sat with Todd on the living room sofa. He moved the phone onto the coffee table. We waited.

It rang again. Night magnified both silence and sound. I could hear Jeff's voice from the receiver, breaking with the news. Bleeding in his brain from the stroke. A matter of time. Come as soon as you can.

In the years that I'd been part of the Harris family, my father-in-law had always been on the periphery of family relationships. At first it seemed to me that his sons misunderstood him. He was a geeky misfit, trying to be loved. He was also an important geneticist with the USDA. He published a thick textbook and presented at conferences in his broad Texas drawl. The classic absent-minded professor, he sometimes left the truck door hanging open when he went in to work. Misplaced keys, driving through red lights, the usual. His wife worried about the open train tracks across the country road he drove home from work. When she found him that morning on the floor, his speech slurred and confused, she knew it was a stroke. She dialed the ambulance.

I ironed Todd's white dress shirt at about 3:00 a.m., my ironing board set up next to the kitchen window. The kitchen light bounced against the window, so in it I saw my reflection, ironing left handed. The mirror me misted each sleeve with a spray bottle, then pressed the iron over the beads of water so they burst and sizzled into a vapor and vanished. Steam from the ironing condensed on the inside of the cold window; the mist gathered into drops until they grew heavy and fell to the windowsill.

"Do you want this on a hanger?" I carried the ironed shirt to the bedroom, where Todd opened and closed drawers, piled underwear and T-shirts on the bed, reached down the suitcase and garment bag from atop the tall wardrobe.

"With my suit," he said. "I need my suit for the funeral. Which tie?" We moved on autopilot. Just doing the next thing.

I sat on the side of the bed with a notepad and pencil, making a list of what needed to be done and who should be notified. I would stay in Jordan with the girls. I was still recovering from a Cesarean delivery; the baby was due for her two-month immunizations in a few days.

By 4:00 a.m., Todd was packed. The baby roused and I nursed her while we waited for first light. With the sunrise Call to Prayer echoing outside, Todd phoned and woke our friend Bryan, who lived on our side of town. Within thirty minutes Bryan pulled up in his yellow Citroen to take Todd to the airport.

"I love you, Babe."

"Love you, too. Be safe."

Todd folded himself into the passenger's seat, and they drove away. The breezeless morning air felt neither warm nor cool. The leaves on the olive trees across the street hung motionless, as if turned to stone.

My eldest daughter had just turned three, with few memories of her grandfather. This was the day we had planned to take her to buy a big-girl bed. It was to be Laurie's shining day—shopping with Daddy and Mommy at the furniture bazaar, lying stretched out on a big-girl bed, posing long and tall and three years old, sending the picture to G-Mom and G-Dad so they could stick it to the fridge with a butterfly magnet.

"Sweetheart, listen to me. We can't go shopping for your bed today. Daddy had to go on an airplane last night to be with G-Dad."

"That's okay, Mama. Can I have hot chocolate?"

"G-Dad is sick, Baby. He can't get better from this sickness, so he's going to die."

As awkward as my father-in-law was, he loved Laurie, the only grandchild he ever knew. When she was a month old, he laid this bundled newborn on his lap and read the same Dr. Seuss book to her over and over again, *Oh, the Places You'll Go!* The summer before he died, when we returned to the U.S. for cooler weather and to visit family, he sprawled on the floor with two-year-old Laurie for an hour, maybe longer, as she plunked pennies into a piggy bank. When she filled the bank and said, "Again!" her grandfather dumped the pennies out of the bank and watched her put them all in again. And again. Never cross with her—not once. He hadn't met our new baby, born in

Jordan, but he taped Ashley's birth announcement up on his office door, right under his nameplate. My children would never know their grandfather. And that meant they would never see his harsh and violent side.

At times he grew angry, especially when his sons spoke of religion. Such conversations came easily to his three sons—an evangelical campus minister, a Presbyterian seminarian, and an evangelical turned Unitarian Universalist. The brothers disagreed on a great many things, but they enjoyed the debate. It didn't seem personal until he entered the room. He forbade talk of religion in his presence. But the boys had outgrown spankings. Despite their father's warnings, they talked about religion. I wished they would let it go and keep the peace.

My father-in-law grew up in Central Texas, in a Primitive Baptist family. The Primitive Baptists are a secretive bunch. The board outside of one Primitive Baptist Church in Texas reads "Visitors Not Welcome." Primitive Baptists believe that God predestined some people to believe the Christian gospel and others to be hardened to it. My father-in-law was never baptized, and by the time he went to college, the study of science answered any remaining questions he held about ultimate truth. His church friends washed their hands of him. He became an outsider. Visitors not welcome.

He married a Methodist girl and attended church with her, as did most of their friends and neighbors in the sixties. He snoozed through sermons. When the babies came, he refused to have them baptized. "We'll raise them to think for themselves," he said.

Religion wasn't threatening to my father-in-law until his sons took it seriously. One by one, as teenagers, the sons came to believe what their father rejected. One by one they were baptized. "I raised my sons to think for themselves," he said, "and I was disappointed when they did."

He no longer snoozed through sermons. He abandoned the church, though intellectually he'd been truant for years. Ennui became hostility. When his teenaged sons went off to church on Sunday mornings, he forbade his wife to attend with them. "We'll study religion at home," he told her. He sat his wife down at the kitchen table and read to her out of the *Encyclopedia Britannica*—entries on Jesus, Christianity, New Testament, and God. She was forbidden to speak of or discuss their readings. After a few Sundays, it was easier not to get out the encyclopedia, and he puttered or napped while his wife slipped *Guideposts* out from under a drawer liner and read her own Sunday morning devotional. There were still fights and anger. Religion wasn't the only topic of disagreement that set him off.

Only once did she come away with bruises. "I fell down the basement stairs," she told her friends. By the time I married into the family, they slept in separate bedrooms. By the time I saw his anger firsthand, I could no longer generate affection for him.

I was pregnant with Laurie the summer we all went out to dinner together at Todd's parents' favorite restaurant. Jeff's girlfriend asked Todd about seminary, and a conversation about spiritual practices developed on our end of the long table. I wished my husband and his two brothers didn't have voices that carried so well—like their father's. He let it go for a few minutes—perhaps out of courtesy to the new girlfriend, who didn't know the family rules. Then his voice erupted, angry and loud. His fist came down. Dishes rattled. Water spilled. People stared. His face blazed. We pushed food around on our plates like chastised children until the waitress gingerly brought the ticket to my father-in-law. We hurried to our separate cars. My mother- and father-in-law drove off. Jeff's girlfriend and Scott's wife wept. I did not cry then. I felt something close to hatred. I wondered how many years it would be before his anger found its way to the child in my womb, who would be baptized and raised in the church. We sat in the restaurant parking lot for a very long time and snuck into the house like teenagers out too late. For the rest of that family visit, when my father-in-law entered the room we slipped away one by one, either physically or emotionally.

I suppose we shunned him, just like the Primitive Baptists. Our relationships weren't natural when he was around. Even before the restaurant scene, he had never really been a part of things. In his own family, surrounded by his sons and their wives, he was an exile.

Bryan told our friends from the expatriate church; his wife set up a meal rotation. Every day a different family stopped by just before suppertime: shepherd's pie from David and Pam; soup and fresh-baked bread from Tom and Melissa. Casseroles and side dishes filled the shelves of my fridge. I froze leftovers and tried to eat for the sake of my breastfeeding infant. I wrote thank-you notes and placed them in the clean pots and platters. There was so much food that I had to throw things away, which for some reason made me cry. My expat friends kept their visits short, seeing that I was busy with the children and that I was easily brought to tears.

Why did I cry? I hardly knew my father-in-law. I didn't like him. But he was my children's grandfather, and to them he had been kind. People can change. I cried for the future, for the death of possibility and hope, however faint.

Tamam sat with me every day while Todd was gone. She came down in the morning in her robe and curlers, and she stopped by when she got home from work, before she started dinner for herself and Dr. Jalal.

"You should wear black," Tamam told me. "People will be so kind to you."

When I crossed the street to buy laundry soap, I wore black. The shop owner never made eye contact and hardly spoke to me most of the time. He closed at prayer times and on Fridays, when I imagined him attending mosque sermons and chanting about the wickedness of the infidel West. But on this day that I wore black, he greeted me. He gave Laurie a lollipop and asked about the baby.

"The father of my husband," I said, not sure of my Arabic for relatives by marriage, "He will die. My husband has gone to America."

"What God has willed," he said and handed me my change.

Two days had passed since the midnight phone call. Would I know when my father-in-law died? It could have already happened, and with the arrangements for cremation, memorial, burial, perhaps I would be forgotten.

Tamam sat on the floor, holding a plastic teacup. I settled myself next to Tamam as Laurie poured and served us imaginary treats. Laurie put her hand on Tamam's arm and said soberly, "My G-Dad is gonna die and I won't ever see him again." She looked pleased with herself for saying something so sophisticated.

Tamam wiped her eyes and I felt emotion rising in my chest.

Tamam understood this in a way my expatriate friends didn't. Because she knew profound loss, she knew how to comfort—by doing and saying little. By being there every day in curlers and by telling me to wear black and by crying with me.

My exile was minor and voluntary—absent from my home country and family of origin, separated from the land by choice. Tamam's exile was the other kind: forced removal. Many Palestinians of the 1948 or 1967 diaspora still hold papers proving their ownership of houses and land in Palestine. They keep the papers sealed in fireproof and waterproof tins, weighted down by the old-fashioned skeleton key to a family home long ago razed by Israeli bulldozers. The keys are handed down to children and grandchildren born in exile so that they remember Palestine, so that they feel the longing to return to her.

Tamam hadn't been much older than Laurie was now when, in 1948, Jewish soldiers seized control of Jerusalem and the surrounding villages. Palestinian Arabs couldn't stay. Along with the neighbors, Tamam's family grabbed a few things and locked the door to their home in Jaba. They fled eastward, eventually finding refuge in Jordan, where the little Palestinian girl became a Jordanian citizen and a wife and a mother, a lecturer in economics. Her grown children, one in college in the U.S., one married to a German and living in Europe, have never seen Palestine, except when they visited Mount Nebo, about an hour south of Amman. In Arabic, the mountain is called *Jabal Moosa*, Moses' Mountain, because from this peak, Moses glimpsed the Promised Land—a land he would never enter. On a clear day, they say, the buildings of Jerusalem reflect the sunlight back across the desert plain of Western Jordan. When I was at Mt. Nebo trying to glimpse the Promised Land, the weather was clear. I saw nothing but haze on the horizon.

"I travel the world to give lectures," said Tamam, "but I can't even get a permit to visit the West Bank. I missed my cousin's wedding, and I have never seen her children. We have to be patient for Palestine. If God wills, someday we will return."

Palestine and her shining daughter Jerusalem have been under siege time and again through history. In the sixth century B.C. the Babylonian army under Nebuchadnezzar destroyed Jerusalem and her Jewish temple. The brightest and best Jews were taken captive and marched across the desert from Palestine to Babylon: into exile. Others fled the conquerors as Tamam's family did and scattered outside of Palestine, settling in Egypt and throughout Assyria.

Those in Babylon became slaves in the great foreign city, some of them living in Nebuchadnezzar's opulent castle, which was far more majestic than the provincial temple in Jerusalem, home to their provincial god. Babylon stood majestic on the banks of the Euphrates River, a luxurious city of wealth, fortified with the booty of conquered nations, with rich tasty foods and glorious art and architecture: the height of civilization.

Before this great fall of Jerusalem to the Babylonians, the prophet Jeremiah warned the Jews. He prophesied that if they didn't wash their hearts from evil, judgment would come at the hand of a great army, which would surround the holy city, speaking in a language they wouldn't understand. "As you have forsaken me and served foreign gods in your land, so you shall serve foreigners in a land that is not yours" (Jer. 5:19).

The great city of Babylon, bowing to foreign gods, mocked the Jews with their holy city of dust and small achievements. The captives were more than homesick. Jerusalem was where their God dwelled, and from him they had been exiled.

When friends brought food they always asked about Todd's dad. I didn't know how to answer them. International long distance was expensive. I fell asleep counting backwards to the time zone in Nebraska, waiting for the phone to ring.

Todd called the evening after it happened. He and Jeff had been with their father in the hospital room at the end. "His breathing was so bad," Todd said. "It got worse and worse and then he was gone."

My father-in-law's exile from the family was permanent.

"My brothers are both speaking at Dad's memorial service," Todd said. "At first I refused. I couldn't think of anything nice to say. Then I thought of him with Laurie. I cried for the first time. He was a good grandfather. So I'll talk about that at the service."

I encouraged Todd to stay on with his mom through Thanksgiving, though it would mean another two weeks for me alone in Jordan. I wanted to be generous and loving, but the truth is I also wanted my husband back. I wished I had packed a suitcase and crowded into Bryan's Citroen that morning. I wished I were back home.

The tile floor in the study was cold, and I felt the chill in my calves and shins beginning to ache. I walked through the silent house, checked on sleeping children, took ibuprofen, and went to bed. I fantasized about flying back to the U.S. to join my husband and in-laws. Because

Todd was staying for Thanksgiving, still two weeks away, maybe it would be reasonable for me to fly back with the girls even now. Wouldn't the presence of children—of a new baby—be a comfort and distraction to everyone at this time? We didn't have the money for more flight tickets, but I had a credit card. Should money drive decisions at a time like this?

Todd called again the day of the service, evening for me—afternoon for him. He and his brothers had each given brief eulogies, and now they enjoyed the time at home with their cousins in the bittersweet reunion that a funeral often brings. I heard the laughter in the background, a world away.

"Is everything okay there, Lisa?"

"Yes. No news here. Tamam is like a sister."

"What was that? Oh, hey. Mom wants to talk to you."

My mother-in-law came on the phone to thank me for sending video of the girls.

"It's so nice to see life right now, to see the baby and how Laurie has grown."

"Oh, Mom. I wish I had come. If the girls and I were there, maybe it would be a comfort—"

"Oh, no dear. Things are so busy. It's just as well. Nice talking to you and I'll pass the phone back to Todd."

"Hey, Babe, gotta go now. We're going out for dinner and we need to get a move on. Bye."

"Bye, Todd."

I hung up the phone and whispered, I miss you.

By the waters of Babylon,
There we sat down and wept,
When we remembered Zion.
——Psalm 137:1

For seventy years the Jewish captives lived in Babylon. I think of them as a people who ached for home, who longed to be reunited with their God. The poet of Psalm 139 paints a picture of exiles weeping on the banks of the Euphrates River, their tears flowing down through Mesopotamia to join the salty water of what is now the Persian Gulf.

I see one captive fall asleep at night with tears of longing. He's not a Bible character—he exists only in my imagination. This man dreams of Zion, the city of God. He wakes at midnight, unsure at first if perhaps it is all a nightmare, until he opens his eyes to the half light of another night in Babylon. Still in slavery. Still exiled. If only he could fly, like dry leaves on the fall wind, back to Jerusalem.

How long, O Lord, will you forget your people? Many of the captives died during those years in Babylon, their bones forever exiled. Did some of them forget their God?

Longing hardens to anger. He will never again worship the God who sent his own chosen people marching across the desert into slavery. He forbids his family to speak of Jerusalem or of her God. That last night in Jerusalem, when Nebuchadnezzar's army broke down the city's walls and flowed in like floodwaters through the breach, the man—a young boy then—stooped to snatch up a stone. But a goliath of a soldier had him chained before he could draw back his arm and take aim. The boy held onto the stone. He brought a piece of the Promised Land out with him and into Babylonia. He kept it to remember his God and his homeland. When his own son, born into slavery, was old enough to understand, he handed it down.

But God has not remembered him. This man's anger erupts whenever he hears talk of Jerusalem or of the God who once claimed a covenant with his people. His sons speak in whispers; they fall silent when their father comes near. One night he grasps the stone of remembrance in his fist and carries it to the banks of the Euphrates. He draws back his arm and takes aim. He hurls it all into the depths.

He knows he will die in exile.

I woke unsure of what day it was, but Todd lay in bed beside me. In the dark of early morning, I got up and put on my slippers.

Todd's flight had arrived around midnight. I sat in the living room waiting for him, holding a book but not reading. I heard a car from a long way off and went to stand in the shadows of the enclosed part of our veranda.

Todd pulled his suitcase from the trunk. He paid the driver through the window, and the taxi drove off before Todd came up the porch stairs. He left his suitcase just inside the door.

"It's so good to be home," he said.

And now he slept while I stood by the bed in the dark, watching him. We needed heat so the girls wouldn't wake to the cold. I slipped through the dark hallway out to the front part of the house and slid the thermostat up a couple of notches. Radiators clunked and ticked as hot water flowed through them to every room in the house.

The living room furnishings were a combination of Tamam's things and mine. Her blue plush couches and chairs formed two clusters of seating in the large room. Standing before the window, I pulled the strap to raise the exterior metal blinds. I spread the lace curtains aside and saw reflected in the window all the artifacts of my life: my daughter's rocking horse, the chair where I sat to nurse my baby, the door to Todd's study. Stepping through the parted lace I shrouded myself from the reflection of my life and looked out. No one roamed the streets at this hour, not dogs or beggars, not neighbors or sanitation workers. The living all had shelter someplace. A ghost on the outside looking in would have seen but a muted reflection of my pale hair and skin: the living looking through a dim glass toward death.

The night wind howled softly. Below the window, a garden grew, colorful in spring and summer, the flowers deadheaded in the fall. To the right of the window, stone steps led from the entrance down through the walled garden to a gate locked shut to protect those inside. The November breeze swept half-decayed leaves across the street where an olive tree stood alone in the blue streetlight. The night wind pushed dead leaves and debris on down the street and drove them out past the city walls and into the desert.

CHAPTER 16

HER FACE CHANGES

We'd been up late for New Year's Eve so when four-month-old Ashley went down for her nap that New Year's Day, I did, too. Sleep suspended me so that I was oblivious to the woman right outside my bedroom window; I heard Todd's running shower only as a distant stream in a peaceful garden.

Todd tells how he got out of the shower, wrapped a towel around his waist, and dripped his way across the tile floor of our bedroom. I floated in the delicious heavy sleep of an afternoon nap. While reaching into his underwear drawer he saw movement out of the corner of his eye and stepped toward the back window. At the same moment a woman bundled against the January cold glanced over to the bedroom window. Then the meeting of eyes and Todd's realization.

"Hey! She's stealing our laundry!"

I jumped awake at Todd's voice and adrenaline displaced languor. Through the window I saw the blur of a woman not five feet away from me. Except for the bars on the window, I could have climbed out after her. Except for his nakedness, Todd would have set out in pursuit. In stocking feet I ran down the hall, through the kitchen, and finally, out the back door. The laundry line rocked like a jump rope, but she was gone. I ran up the hill, nearly barefoot in the cold, knowing she couldn't have gone far. Soon Todd was dressed and off in the opposite direction. Our neighbor joined the chase around the block until we all met in front of the house, breathing hard. She'd gotten away.

She held a large sack, Todd remembered, and a boy stood guard for her a few meters from the clothesline, out where our yard stood open to the driveway. Our neighbor had seen a boy carrying a large sack just up the block but hadn't confronted him, because we'd said the thief was a woman. Never mind. Too late to catch her. Too late to get back whatever she'd stolen from us. So sorry, the neighbor said, but the poor are like that, you know.

My hands shook as I took down the remaining laundry and made an inventory. She'd taken Ashley's four blanket sleepers—all we had were out with the wash—and she even took the clothespins. Very efficient. Surely she would have worked her way through the rest of the clean clothing if she hadn't seen Todd watching her. We needed a fence around the yard, a lock. But these things wouldn't get back Ashley's pajamas.

January nights are cold, even in the Middle East, and Ashley kicked off her blankets and woke with icy toes and fingers. I lifted her from the crib and tried to wrap my robe around both of us. There in the dark, rocking Ashley back to sleep, her small cold fingers against my skin, I replayed the day's scene. Why, I wondered as I fell asleep with Ashley in my arms, why even the clothespins?

The next day I went downtown where refugee Iraqi widows in black robes spread their mats along the cold sidewalk, lining up bundles of winter herbs, or cheap plastic sandals. Some sat on the pavement with nothing to sell and hands outstretched for coins. I walked past all of them to the secondhand bazaar where I often shopped for my own shoes—good Italian leather boots or pumps that needed only to be reheeled for a few cents. But this time I walked by the open stalls with shoes hung bundled on straps like braids of garlic. I dug through tables and bins of used clothing, looking for sleepers in any size. I asked shopkeeper after shopkeeper if a poor woman had come trying to sell baby clothes. I fantasized that the thief would show and that I would catch her. Even as I envisioned the confrontation, I knew I was daydreaming. I wouldn't find her again, but maybe I could buy a used blanket sleeper at one of the stalls.

I found no fleece sleepers for sale, not even in the wrong size. I took a taxi to the west side of Amman, closer to home, where the wealthy shopped. There the streets were less crowded and merchandise was sold inside clean shops with glass doors. A shop owner wearing a Western necktie greeted me in English as I entered his store. Crisp pastel sailor suits hung on pegs alongside ruffled baby dresses with matching panties—imported from France, the shop owner boasted. Near the rear of the shop leather shoes from Germany sat displayed neatly on a carefully constructed tower of tiny shoeboxes. Infant pajamas cost more than forty dollars a pair.

I walked out empty-handed to hail a taxi home, but not because I couldn't afford the overpriced blanket sleepers. Poverty didn't make my decision for me. I *chose* to do without.

At bedtime that night, and for all the nights that followed, I let Ashley wear her onesie and her stretchsuit to bed. I added layers of clothing, everyday clothing, each night until my child no longer woke to the midnight cold.

Ashley slept the rest of the winter layered and warm, with her dresser drawers full—plenty to wear the next day, and the next, whether I got laundry done or not. Between the laundry line and the driveway stood a newly constructed fence of shiny chicken wire stretched onto a wood frame. We bought a padlock for its gate, and I again hung laundry on the backyard line. At times I thought I heard footsteps in the backyard, though I knew none trespassed now. I found myself thinking new thoughts that prevented me from napping in the afternoons.

I'd never before wondered how the poor kept their children warm at night. Did she live close to us—maybe in one of those dingy flats up over the butcher shop? Was she one of the Bedouin from the bundle of tents and pickups in the empty lot at the end of our street? I'd never recognize her if I saw her again, glazed as my eyes had been that day, with sleep . . . and with anger. As weeks passed and my baby slept warm, my self-righteous anger was converted to curiosity, and sometimes compassion.

Perhaps her sins weighed on her, the shame of teaching her son to steal making her avert her eyes even from her own child's face. Or maybe the weight lifted once her baby was warm at night. What would be the greater moral burden—a shivering baby who refuses to be comforted night after night, or the memory of a quick pull of a garment off the laundry line and a dash to safety? I continued to daydream of catching her in the act, but my imagination now had me receiving her with understanding.

I thought about her all winter, through the hard rains and gloomy days and the one snowfall. I thought of her as the woman without a face, a rush of eyes and scarf and skirts outside my bedroom window. And I thought of her baby, now sleeping warm.

My own child grew. Ashley sat up without support
and learned to crawl on tile floors. When spring warmed
the house and desert winds blew, we began to keep the
windows open and we mopped more frequently. Even so,
we bathed Ashley every day, soaping the dirt off her knees
and the tops of her bare feet. When we went out for a walk
I pushed the stroller past the Bedouin camp at the end of
the street. One time a grubby little girl waved at me without smiling. In the tent behind her woven carpets lay right
over the dirt. I saw no baby clothes there, though I didn't
care so much by that time. The Bedouin packed up and left
before the weather got hot, but through every season the
changing faces of the poor we always had with us.

It was a hot day when the old woman came to me. I had a
houseful of guests that morning, and I nearly missed her,
except that I dashed into the kitchen just then to refill the
creamer before returning to the conversations that wove
English words through my living room.

So I heard her, hardly knocking, almost scratching at
the side door. Her eyes swam behind thick glasses, and she
wore a scarf tied babushka-style under her chin. I couldn't
understand the toothless Arabic she spoke in syllables
without consonants. I gave her water; she drank, perspira-
tion beading on her forehead. She wiped the moisture with
one of the tails from her scarf. I offered her a chair, but she
refused. My guests ate and drank, talked and laughed in
the front of the house.

I poured more bottled water into her glass and looked
frantically for something else, something extra to give this
woman. In the freezer were cubes of homemade baby food.

They would be perfect for the toothless woman. I hesitated, the frozen air chilling my face. No . . . baby food would be too strange a gift; she wouldn't understand. But I had to give her more than water. I shifted the cubes to pull out a package of minced lamb. When I handed her the second glass of water, I slipped the meat into her purse. She felt the tug and pulled the purse away, but I told her in Arabic that I was giving and not taking. Through the thick glasses, her eyes didn't seem to focus. Looking past me—or through me, it seemed—she thanked in vowels, and she blessed. I walked her out to the street, my hand under her elbow. She asked me something like, "Which way to the east?" Then she walked in the direction I indicated, and I returned to my friends.

No one asked me where I'd been. My guests hadn't seen the old woman at my back door. Like all the poor in my life, she was there and then she was gone.

Ashley is ten now and doesn't remember living in the Middle East. She rides with me to where the frontage road curves, near the liquor store, where day after day we've seen a homeless man perched on the guardrail holding a cardboard sign. We usually drive right past him—but yesterday we stopped. The weatherman said the high temperature would be near one hundred. It's as hot as July, though it's still early spring, so yesterday we brought him two gallon jugs filled with ice water. He poured for his dog before he lifted the jug to take a drink himself. Today it's hot again and we've brought more water. But this time he's gone.

We leave the water jugs under a tree and get back in the car.

I blast the air conditioning for our ride home, and I glance in the rearview mirror. Ashley gazes out the side window, off past the liquor store. When I look back to the road, I see her face reflected in the windshield. Ashley looks like me. Does she think the thoughts I do? Does she wonder where the homeless man is and whether he's thirsty? We drive back to the house through heat that creates mirages of water pooling on the road, always just ahead, there and then gone.

Once home, Ashley slips in the front door ahead of me, and in the moment it takes me to close and lock the door, she's upstairs and out of sight. She's probably writing in her diary, I think as I hang my keys on the kitchen peg. Or she's daydreaming, imagining that the homeless man has returned to his spot by the guardrail and is drinking from one of the water jugs before the ice melts.

Sometimes I imagine a light knock at my door—I see movement in the back yard or the laundry line swaying like a swing when a child jumps from it and runs away. Now my mind makes her a composite of the Bedouin girl, the thirsty old woman, the mother desperate to keep her child warm at night. So her face changes, my memory is altered, and I see my own child pleading at a back door for warm clothing and a glass of water.

CHAPTER 17

WILD OLIVE SHOOT

News crossed the city in urgent rumors, from courtyard to courtyard, over produce carts piled with tomatoes and cucumbers—from the dusty, poor neighborhoods on the outskirts of the city all the way to Al Baraka Palace, where Queen Noor's grandchildren were safe in their royal nursery.

Did you hear?

At the hospital—a terrible thing.

What Allah has willed!

The nurse went to bring a baby to his mother. She found the crib was empty.

Oh, that poor mother!

Never worry. They will find the baby.

Allah is merciful and compassionate.

Yes, they will find the child. The kidnapper will be too ashamed.

At this news I thought I felt my third child flutter within me—but that was impossible; I'd only learned I was pregnant a few days earlier. When Ashley was born I felt such a confidence in the Arabic hospital. I was the only Caucasian mother in the maternity ward, and Ashley was the fairest baby. I never wondered whether they'd brought

me the wrong child. I never worried that she might be
kidnapped from her hospital bassinet.

In the afternoons while Laurie and Ashley rested, I
napped. Those naps sabotaged my nighttime sleep, so
when the house was dark and the rest of my family slept,
I lay awake and thought of babies. My own unborn child,
the size of a grain of rice, would either grow or die. My
sister-in-law Michelle, married to Todd's brother and living in Africa, would soon be an adoptive mother. She and
Scott had decided on international adoption, most likely
from Asia or Latin America. When I finally fell asleep
I dreamed of babies, dark-skinned and fair: fetal, kidnapped, abandoned.

My morning sickness passed. The baby's heartbeat blipped
clearly on the ultrasound screen at my three-month appointment. And still the stolen baby had not been found.

A friend, an American nurse serving in a missionary
hospital south of Amman, came to visit me. She carried a
bundled newborn. A Bedouin girl gave birth to little Mohammed, she told me, running her finger along the side
of his cheek. He weighed less than six pounds and had
some minor health trouble. With nurture he would grow as
hearty as any other baby. The birth mother wouldn't hold
her small son. She seemed relieved when the staff pediatrician told her that the baby should stay in the hospital until
he was stronger. The Bedouin girl slipped out before the
admissions nurse brought her the proper forms.

Mohammed's face was perfectly round, his fingers long
and graceful. He didn't hold his hands in fists the way
most newborns do, remembering with their bodies the

tight space they so recently inhabited. It was as if Mohammed had already set about the business of forgetting his
mother's womb.

When my friend offered to take him home with her,
the night nurse thanked her. He would have someone to
mother him for a few days. It sometimes happened this
way, my friend said, smoothing his flyaway hair. The Bedouin bury their dead in the shifting sands. They live in
tents with no running water.

"A child like this will grow up in an orphanage," my
friend told me. "It's a matter of weeks."

In Jordan an abandoned child is a ward of the state.
Regardless of parentage he is assigned a Muslim name and
sent to a Muslim orphanage. There are no adoption agencies in Jordan. Even if his Bedouin birth mother had filled
out the proper forms at the hospital, Mohammed's birth
certificate would be fictionalized—the original destroyed
and his history erased once he was fully abandoned. The
Ministry of the Interior's Department of Civil Status would
reissue a birth certificate with false names for mother and
father, and a new name for the child. The names would be
chosen at random, and this boy would never know that he
was a child of the Bedouin.

I held Mohammed and placed my finger against his
open palm. He wrapped his long fingers around mine and
held tight. What talents do long fingers promise? Was this
child to be a sculptor, a pianist, a weaver? I'd asked such
questions of my own tight-fisted newborns as I whispered a
mother's promises to them: you will have stories and music
and love. But what promises could I give this abandoned
child? I pictured his long name written down the length
of his body, the last letters falling off when the writing
reached his toes and ran out of baby. Such a small canvas,
such a big name.

Mohammed sucked his bottom lip as he slept, and in that pulsing I saw my own babies at my breast. Whether by bottle or breast this child needed a mother to feed him. He whimpered, from what dream or absence of dream, I could not know.

"Hush, baby," I said. "Be still."

I thought again of my sister-in-law, Michelle, still childless, still waiting. Michelle possessed in her own long fingers a talent for sketching and watercolor painting. Mohammed's dark hair was the same shade as hers. Hadn't Michelle told me that adoption agencies often use photos of the prospective parents to match a child physically to his adoptive family?

I loved the fall season in Jordan. There were no stunning color changes, no familiar triggers of autumn nostalgia. To love a Jordanian fall I had to receive it according to Arab standards and not my own.

The nights grow cooler toward the end of August and even in the hottest part of a late August day in Jordan there's an edge of something in the air—a promise of refreshing. In the mornings particularly, the tap water runs cold again, drawn from a rooftop or backyard tank. The children go back to school in September all crisp and equalized in their smock uniforms. That fall, when I was expecting a third child and dreaming of babies not my own, I took long walks up and down the hilly streets of our neighborhood. We lived on the same street as the American School in Amman, and the guard in his booth at the entrance nodded at me as I walked by. I stopped to watch the children in the fenced field as they ran and shouted.

Arabs and Europeans, Asians and Americans kicked a ball down a level field. The boy with the almond eyes had Asian ancestry—but he easily might be American, I thought. The dark girl with her hair coiled like the crown of African royalty might carry a passport from almost anywhere. These children had every opportunity not because they'd achieved but because they'd been born—or perhaps adopted—into families that could offer them the best.

Where would Mohammed go to school? If he belonged to the right family, he might be on this very playground in ten years. More likely he would be eating beans and bread off a tin plate in an institution.

I stood in the partial shade of a low olive tree. The olives were still hard and green, like tight-fisted fetuses, but they would be black and ready for picking by November.

The cultivated olive tree bears fruit with a thick layer of flesh surrounding a small pit. It contains more precious oil than its cousin, the wild olive. Although the fruit it bears is hardly worth harvesting, the wild olive tree is scrubby and tough, with a reputation like the Bedouin. For thousands of years farmers in the Middle East have been grafting cultivated olive shoots onto wild olive trees to channel the vigor of the wild root into the fruit of the cultivated branch.

As I walked home from the American School that day past the many olive trees planted along my street, I thought of myself as that cultivated olive shoot, grafted on to the wild tree of life in the Middle East.

What about Mohammed? He was a wild olive shoot, cut off from his Bedouin source through no fault of his own, still young and fresh. A wild shoot is never grafted into the cultivated olive tree. Never. Any Arab who tends olive trees would scorn the suggestion of it. The concept is upside-down and foolish, against nature.

In Islam an orphan cannot be adopted into a family whose blood is not his own any more than a fruitless wild shoot can be grafted onto a cultivated tree. Islamic law forbids legal adoption. An orphan may have guardians, but under the law a child will not receive the name of the guardian family because he does not share in their blood. Likewise, he is not permitted to receive any inheritance, no matter how small. The family name and legacy are passed down to birth children only.

King Hussein himself took in a wild olive shoot, called his "adopted daughter" by foreign journalists who don't understand the laws of Jordan. "She kept her own name," wrote one American reporter, as if this young woman were free and liberated and had made the choice herself. King Hussein, while he lived, called this child his daughter. But she is not a princess. She is not an heir. The king obeys the laws of his own land and religion, those controlling ordinances that are higher, older, deeper than his own monarchy. By whatever name the Jordanian royal family calls their wild olive shoot, she is not fully grafted in.

Michelle and I like to say that by marrying brothers, we became sisters. Like a younger sister, Michelle has followed close behind, as if to overtake me at each threshold. I said yes to Todd's marriage proposal in May; Michelle said yes to Scott in July of that same year. My wedding was in August; Michelle's was in December. When I became pregnant with my first child, I expected that Michelle would be just a few months behind.

When we all met years ago in Nebraska for a family reunion I confided in Michelle that Todd and I had timed the pregnancy in order to have the first baby in the States, before we moved to the Middle East. Michelle confided back to me that she and Scott were now "trying." With great anticipation I bought Michelle the classic book on what to expect in pregnancy and childbearing. I presented it to her behind closed doors, and she slipped it under some jeans in her suitcase. We were both embarrassed and hopeful, dreaming of cousins who would be best friends across the miles.

It has been thirteen years since I bought that book for Michelle in a Nebraska bookstore. My eldest child and hers are the closest of friends, though they are nearly five years apart in age with eighteen inches difference in their height. Laurie is blond and fair; Michelle's son is olive-skinned and dark. Like their mothers, these cousins enjoy a friendship as close as if they were related by blood.

By the time I held Mohammed and felt my own third child stretching in my womb, Michelle had watched me through two pregnancies, reading and rereading her preparation for pregnancy book until it was as well worn as my own copy. She took it with her to Central Africa where she taught first grade at an international school while Scott worked at the university. Michelle signed teaching contracts year after year, making promises to other women's children. Michelle's hopes were thwarted by infertility, her longings watered by waiting, the same way Ramadan fasting makes one not oblivious to food and water, but more desperate for it.

In Jordan, Mohammed waited in a forced fast from the love of a mother. Once the Ministry of the Interior recreated his birth certificate with false names it would be too late. Soon Mohammed's window of opportunity would be sealed shut.

I've always been a fixer—like when good friends in college had a crush on each other, neither knowing for sure what the other felt. I didn't do much except encourage him to ask her out and her to wait patiently until he did. Still, they asked me to stand up at their wedding and tell the story of how I'd been their matchmaker.

In a different culture I'd have been a *yenta*. Thing is, when Gentiles learn their Yiddish from musical theater, they don't get the meanings straight. *Yenta* doesn't mean matchmaker at all. It means someone who meddles or gossips. A busybody.

With Michelle it was a different issue. A different kind of matchmaking. Nature wasn't working right and no babies came. Michelle taught her first graders that birds lay eggs and that honeybees shelter their young in waxy cells. At the end of the year the mother of a petite French child came to Michelle saying, you love the children so. You should be a mother. Michelle thanked the woman and gave her a handwritten report card. It was too soon to tell anyone that they were planning to adopt. Once they'd decided on an agency and were accepted, then it would be time to tell. So perhaps I wasn't fixing so much as I was trying to be a midwife to an adoptive mother—I came alongside in the process that was already under way.

I felt like a child the night before Christmas as I typed out the email to Michelle telling her about Mohammed and how children like him had no hope of growing up in a family. Not officially. But there were ways. I only had a few more questions to ask, but it seemed workable. It could happen by the time you come to Jordan for Christmas, I wrote. You could have a baby like Mohammed in your arms by the New Year.

Find out the details, she wrote back. We can't go breaking laws to adopt a child, but find out if it could work.

The possibility that I could have a role in the adoption made me feel a new bond with Michelle. I had long suspected that the news of each of my pregnancies stung her, like I'd cut in line once again. And each time we announced another pregnancy I wondered if we should have waited, allowing Scott and Michelle the honor of being father and mother to the next Harris grandchild before we produced another and then another.

I didn't tell Michelle how my nurse friend had lowered her voice when she explained that we would have to act before the government created a new birth certificate for the child, how she'd warned me not to discuss the issue over the phone because sometimes the lines are tapped. The situation required caution and discretion. My friend said to find an obstetrician who would falsify birth records. That was the key. With a birth record we could bring the baby to the embassy, apply for passport and social security card, and the child would be indelibly part of his new family.

Night after night while Todd and the girls slept I lay in the dark and developed the entire scenario—to a point. As we'd done with our birth children, we would take Mohammed to the embassy to apply for his passport. All we needed was a birth certificate, a copy of our own marriage license, and the baby. If I could do it before my own pregnancy started to show very much it would be easier, in case there were questions at the embassy. Or we could wait and have my doctor list the adopted baby as the twin to my birth child. At my next obstetric appointment I would ask. I couldn't come right out and ask my doctor to falsify records, but I could raise the topic and wait for him to propose the solution, the Arab way. Once the birth certificate was arranged, Mohammed would be ours.

There were just a few details left to work out, most prominent perhaps was how to officially make the baby Scott and Michelle's instead of mine. But that could all happen back home, I thought sleepily. The most important thing would be to get the baby into my arms as soon as possible. From there any remaining details would fall into place.

As my pregnancy progressed I looked with envy on the conservative Muslim women from the other side of town, because they wore shapeless robes that were comfortable during pregnancy. I only knew of one American woman who wore those traditional robes: her husband was an Egyptian and a member of the Muslim brotherhood. Perhaps if we still lived on the outskirts of Amman I could have gotten away with it—but not in this part of town. I had to dress to fit in with my sophisticated Arab neighbors and avoid looking like a fundamentalist Muslim convert. From the secondhand bazaar I bought stretch pants and elastic-waisted skirts and I sewed looser elastic into each waistband. I borrowed a sewing machine and added fabric gussets along the side seams of my tops so that they would fit.

The hospital kidnapper was one of those women in the shapeless robes, it turned out. And she was infertile. Next to fornication or adultery, infertility causes the greatest loss of honor for a Muslim woman. A husband may divorce or take a second wife in order to ensure that there will be children. Babies are a measure of family honor and standing in the community—especially baby boys.

The reports made it sound as if the prowess of the Jordanian police force was responsible for solving the crime. In fact the kidnapper's family solved the mystery themselves when they put two and two together and saw that it didn't add up to nine months. Family honor was too important. They came forward.

The woman—we'll call her Zahra—had been married a few years but was childless. Zahra's in-laws and husband insisted that her infertility didn't matter; her husband loved her. The marriage was safe, but Zahra felt ashamed that she hadn't been able to produce a child. Though her husband loved her, the neighbors talked. Even after the baby came, they talked. Some said that Zahra had been violent with the child. Someone said there were bloodstains on the cement floors of Zahra's modest home.

I don't know which details were fabricated through rumor and which emerged through the course of the investigation. There were so many versions. The story I heard most often was that one day Zahra came cradling a newborn. She confessed to her mother-in-law how she concealed the pregnancy, afraid that she would miscarry. So she hid the pregnancy under her robes until the labor pains came. The baby was born at home on a straw mat over the cement floor, she told them. She cut the cord herself with shears she'd bought from the barber. The account she told her husband differed—she'd cut the cord with a kitchen knife then used rags and water to clean up the blood. Her in-laws and husband loved the new baby. At first they said that Zahra's confusion meant nothing. She was exhausted after nine months of hiding and then giving birth alone. She needed their help.

"It is difficult," he said. "I don't know of anything like this."

My obstetric appointments started in the doctor's study outside of his examining room. I sat across the desk from him, and we discussed my pregnancy and any concerns or developments. When time came for the examination, he buzzed for his nurse, who met me in the exam room. She weighed me and got me set up modestly under a sheet for the exam, which was always by ultrasound with the doctor's eyes on the screen and not on me. Both of my "Jordan babies" were born by Cesarean section and I used to joke that from the first appointment to the birth and the six-week follow up my doctor never touched me. A male obstetric doctor in a conservative culture, he remained above reproach.

During the desk consultation before the ultrasound—while we were alone—I raised the question of unwanted or orphaned babies. I explained that my sister-in-law wanted to adopt, and I asked how one would go about things in Jordan.

"It is very difficult," he said, looking over toward the door as if his receptionist were due to enter the office. "I don't know of any such a case."

This doctor had looked me straight in the eye when he told me that my rice-sized baby didn't seem to be growing. "No sex for a month," he'd said without breaking eye contact. How was it that theoretical talk of adoption made him avert his eyes and want to change the subject when his entire practice was about speaking the difficult things related to infertility and childbirth?

"It is difficult" is a nice Arab way of saying "It will never happen."

I understood. There was no asking him to falsify birth records. He wasn't going to offer, and I knew not to ask again. Was it so sneaky? And why did it matter if it was? When I thought about a child being brought up in an orphanage instead of in our extended family, the greater good seemed obvious.

Michelle knew better. Even longing for a child as she did, she wouldn't bite. "We just can't do it this way, Lisa."

And so my fantasy ended. Mohammed was strong now; it would not be long before he was taken to an orphanage with a new name and his Bedouin identity erased. There were many abandoned children in Jordan . . . but no lawful way to take them home.

Across town, Zahra's mother-in-law was delighted. Allah placed in her aging arms the child of her prayers: a grandson. But something itched at the grandmother. Something told her that the story wasn't true. How could Zahra have hidden her growing belly for so long? The mother-in-law could not remember Zahra complaining about morning sickness, increased hunger, tiredness, or any of the symptoms she remembered from her own pregnancies. Perhaps Zahra's pregnancy had been easy because the baby was so perfect.

Some nights Zahra left the baby with her mother-in-law all night long. The baby made Zahra tired, so tired. She needed rest. Zahra did not breastfeed, because she still felt heavy with sorrow from her years of infertility, and a neighbor—she couldn't remember who—said that a mother's sorrow would pass from her breast milk into the baby. It wasn't so strange, the mother-in-law told herself. Everything could be explained.

One night as the mother-in-law prepared a bottle, her husband came to the kitchen and spoke to her in a low voice. She told him he was wrong, that he should be ashamed for thinking such a thing about the wife of his own son. But when the mother-in-law handed the bottle to Zahra, saying it might be too hot, she saw that Zahra didn't test the temperature before plunging the nipple into the baby's mouth. It must have felt like a slap in the face. It must have been hard to do what was legal and right—hard to let that baby go.

The authorities came, and when the official reached for the child, Zahra let the baby go and wrapped her empty arms about her own chest, rocking back and forth. So I heard from my neighbors.

Then Zahra told the truth.

For weeks she walked by the hospital every day, sometimes stopping to sit on the bench outside the front doors. Finally she entered the building and stood before the elevator, next to the sign that told her the maternity ward was on the third floor. She only wanted to see the babies that day, Zahra said, perhaps rub a small cloth against the head of a newborn boy for the blessing.

The elevator doors opened. A young mother stood holding a newborn; Zahra moved aside to let them off the elevator. The baby sneezed three times, Zahra remembered. The new mother must not have kept it warm enough. The mother carried a large satchel over one arm. She shifted the baby into the crook of the arm that held the satchel. With her free hand she opened the satchel to reach for something. Zahra saw how easily, how perfectly a newborn could fit into a large purse. She returned another day with her own large satchel.

So the neighbor lady was right. When she told me that *they* would find the baby, I thought she meant the police. She knew—though I didn't—that *they* were the family of the kidnapper, and that *they* would seek honor. The same desire that motivated the kidnapping also inspired the baby's return.

My own yearnings and plans for taking Mohammed, or another orphan, into my family never seemed as horrifying as stealing a baby out of the hospital nursery. But we were alike, Zahra and I. We both wanted a baby who wasn't ours and we were both creative to the point of deception. Neither of us considered the child or the future. Neither of us thought like a mother.

When I went to the hospital to give birth, I wanted my newborn daughter to stay with me. My pediatrician shook her head when I asked about it. She told me no, the baby was safer in the nursery.

"Sometimes things happen," she said. "What if someone comes into your room while you're sleeping? It's very rare, but we want to be cautious."

I was determined. In my hospital bag I carried a set of sleigh bells, dug out from the Christmas box for this use. Todd hung the bells on the door to my hospital room, so that when my pediatrician came in, she laughed and told me she thought she was entering a barbershop.

"All right, then," she said. "I will tell the nurses to leave this baby with her mother."

Once again, Michelle rejoiced for me. With empty arms, she looked motherhood full in the eyes. It was easier for her this time, I think. The adoption paperwork was completed, and the only thing left was the waiting.

Six weeks later in Bogota, Colombia, another woman gave birth in another hospital. The young mother named her son John Edison, thinking the name sounded American. John Edison. Such a long name for such a tiny canvas. He was less than six pounds, but he would grow strong, the nurses assured his birth mother.

The young mother left the hospital with empty arms. If she came back within six weeks, she could reclaim her child with no questions asked. The orphanage workers were sure she wouldn't return. But they waited the weeks required by law and then faxed a picture of John Edison to his adoptive parents. It was time for Scott and Michelle to go to Colombia and bring back their son.

They scooted the name John over to make room for a new first name, and Justin John Harris is the son, the grandson, the best-friend cousin we waited and longed for. Islamic law prohibits the full adoption of its orphans. To graft in a wild olive shoot to the cultivated tree contradicts the logic of horticulture. But no matter how impossible it seems to the botanist or the Islamic scholar, those things were turned upside-down when this Colombian boy was grafted into our family.

It is spring now—past the season for grafting. Angry thunderstorms pound at the windows, sometimes tearing branches from trees or knocking down the fences that divide one family's yard from the next. My window looks out to the backyard and beyond, to the trees that grow in the empty lot on the far side of our back fence. Those trees belong to no one, but their branches stretch over our yard to provide summer shade to my family, a free gift to us who neither cultivate nor tend.

It is yet early in the season. The branches are only now sending out the shoots that will spread leafy fingers against the summer sun. For the past two weeks I have watched new buds push out from the branch, tightly coiled like the fists of a newborn. As I think about Mohammed, I find myself hoping for a storm, thinking that if one of these branches were broken off I would bring it into my household. I would place the broken end in water and watch for it to send out roots. If it should grow I would plant and tend, water and cultivate. Even now, in my midlife, I still imagine myself a savior. Justin's adoption and that of his little sister happened without my help. I should have learned by now.

The tree in the empty lot behind us holds tight to her shoots this year, so there are no botanical orphans for me to rescue. Each tight-fisted bud unfurls into lacy green fingers. Over my backyard a generation of leafy hands dance, bending and bowing to the wind, the rain, and all the forces they must obey.

I speak as to an orphaned babe in my arms. Hush, my soul. Be still.

CHAPTER 18

Wars and
Rumors of Wars

Todd's mom was with us when we heard about the bombing. Our home in Amman was four hours from the Iraq border, eighteen from Baghdad, but still. Jeanne's hands shook as she cut cucumbers in my kitchen—and if I can be quite honest, she was in the bathroom at least three times each hour.

Jeanne had flown in to have Christmas with us, perhaps even go to Bethlehem since we were just a few hours' drive from the Holy Land. Scott and Michelle would arrive from Central Africa in a few days. That was the plan before President Clinton ordered air strikes over Iraq. Now we weren't sure. During the first Gulf War, the airport closed down almost immediately when U.S. air strikes started. Jordanians taped their windows in case any missiles lost their way and fell over Jordan. We didn't live in Jordan at that time, but we'd heard the stories from those who did.

We woke that morning to read from CNN online that Operation Desert Fox had started just after midnight. Tony Blair was the first to speak. The quarrel wasn't with the Iraqi people, he said at a press conference, but with their leader and his evil regime.

When we turned on the English-language news, Jordanian coverage was of happenings in Israel, not in Iraq. Over in the West Bank, Palestinians protested the American aggression in Iraq. Little boys hurled rocks toward the Israeli police. But the soldiers didn't shoot. They held up clear plastic shields and stood shoulder to shoulder, staring straight ahead.

One skinny Palestinian teen with a checkered *koufiyye* wrapped over his head and mouth held a broomstick; from it hung a bulby-nosed Clinton dummy. I had to chuckle at that nose and the straw stuffing coming out around the president's ankles—then the skinny kid held a lighter close to Clinton's knobby foot, and my president went up in flames.

Lots of times I saw American flags burned during Middle East protests—and years later I would watch from the U.S. with the rest of the world while Saddam's own effigy was torn down—broken off at the knees, or just about. But only that once did I see my own leader symbolically destroyed. I clicked the TV off. Jeanne hurried to the bathroom.

This first day of the bombing campaign was also the day of my twenty-week ultrasound. There was no news of anti-American protests in Amman, so Todd and I left Jeanne with the girls and drove through deserted streets to the doctor's office. It felt like a Ramadan sunset when everyone's gone home to break the fast and the streets are empty. It was the kind of morning I remember from my Southern California childhood—brilliant blue sky and warm sun and silent streets with all the big kids off at school. In Amman that first morning of bombs over Baghdad, no one was out shopping or walking or visiting—folks stayed home, watching the news, taping their windows, waiting to see what would come next.

We were the only patients in the waiting room, but the doctor was in. He didn't say a thing about the bombing. The baby's legs were crossed so we had to wait for another appointment to find out that she'd be Jessica and not Jonathan. On the drive back we saw only one other car.

When we got home, Scott called from Africa.

"We've been checking the news. How are things there?"

"Quiet. It feels bizarre."

"Should we come? I mean, what are the chances that the airport will close?"

"We're the last to know anything. As of today the airport is open. Anti-American protests in Israel, though."

"Doesn't matter. We're coming to see you guys and Mom. The trip to Israel isn't the main thing."

"Seems to me the worst that could happen is that the airport would close and you'd be stuck here for a while. But we'd be together."

"That's what we think, too. We'd be together. So . . . we'll see you tomorrow, then."

"We'll be here."

It was like deciding to go ahead and drive to Grandma's for Thanksgiving, even though there might be a big ice storm later in the evening. The weatherman is often wrong about these things.

A few days passed and not a single Iraqi missile flew through Jordanian airspace. Jeanne's hands became steady as she spread peanut butter and jelly on flat Arabic bread to make sandwiches for the girls. The U.S. was still bombing the neighbors, but Jordanians were back on the streets and everyone was feeling more at ease. So far so good. Jeanne went with Todd to meet Scott and Michelle's flight, while I dragged a sleeping mat into the playroom for Todd and me and put fresh sheets on our bed for Scott and Michelle.

The last Christmas we'd spent all together was just before we left Jeanne alone in North America—one brother to Hawaii, one to Africa, the other to the Middle East. We had just Laurie back then, the only grandchild. Now Todd and I had two daughters and Jeff and Carolyn in Hawaii had one—with another two grandchildren on the way soon, one by birth for us and one by adoption for Scott and Michelle.

When they all arrived back from the airport, I asked Todd if there had been extra security.

"Nah. Everything seems normal." And it did. Just like that last Christmas in Nebraska, we were all together in one house. In many ways it felt the same, except when we looked out the window and saw olive trees instead of Nebraska cornfields.

The second night of Ramadan the Jalals invited all of us upstairs to break the fast with them.

"Welcome to the beautiful Middle East," Dr. Jalal said. "I hear you're planning a visit to Israel?"

"We're not sure now—with the protests."

"It will be fine," Tamam said. "I'm sure things will calm down soon."

She went to the kitchen to refill a beverage pitcher, her heels tapping across the tile. We sat in silence, none of us wanting to address U.S. military action in Iraq. Individual Arabs always seemed to understand that while we were American, we had no vote on American military action;

we were neither responsible nor accountable. Then there were the protests where group fervor swept individuals along in a tide of burning effigies and rock throwing. During the first Gulf War, Westerners living in Amman stayed in their homes and had neighbors do their marketing for them in order to stay off the streets.

"If anti-American protests come to Jordan," Dr. Jalal said "You will come upstairs and live in our home. Don't worry; you'll be safe with us. Sometimes these people—they get a little crazy."

We were the only foreigners in the neighborhood, and a flat on the ground floor might not be the best place for us in case of trouble. I wished he hadn't said it in Jeanne's presence, though. We'd have liked her to think we were raising the grandchildren in a safe, though exotic, locale.

Tamam returned from the kitchen. "I hear that the Israelis distributed gas masks today, in case Saddam sends a bomb over to Tel Aviv," she said.

Anti-American protests weren't the only thing we had to worry about.

In those days, it wasn't just the American president and British prime minister who suspected Saddam of those biological weapons that were never found. Certainly the Israelis did. Even the Arabs who defended Iraq's sovereignty knew that Saddam was capable of mass destruction.

"Jordan can't afford such things as gas masks," Tamam continued. "But we are in more danger here."

Because Jordan lies between Iraq and Israel and because Saddam's response to U.S. military force was to threaten his closer enemy, Israel, Jordanians felt defenseless. If Saddam started lobbing missiles over toward Israel and the bombs fell short, they would land in Jordanian streets.

"Jerusalem is lovely," Tamam said. "There will always be a protest in the West Bank, always violence in Palestine. These times are no different than any other times. You should go because you can."

So we went.

CHAPTER 19

O JERUSALEM, JERUSALEM

Our taxi ascended the Mount of Olives. As we reached the crest of the hill I leaned over and peered out the window for my first glimpse of Jerusalem. The gold rotunda of the Dome of the Rock gleamed like an empress's crown.

That golden dome, visible in any panorama of modern Jerusalem, forms a pavilion sheltering the exposed bedrock of Mount Moriah. On that mountain Father Abraham took up the knife to slaughter his son. And there, centuries later, a temple priest took up the blade to circumcise the eight-day-old child of Joseph and Mary.

Muslims believe the Prophet Mohammed ascended on a ladder of light from this holy hill into the very presence of Allah. Now three faiths squabble over who's king of the mountain in a version of the game where all is fair play. But the winner never gets the girl. Boys on one side throw stones to win her. On the other, they grow up to carry machine guns. Tension holds things together it seems, in a city who brings death to her children.

In Arabic, Jerusalem is *Al Quds:* The Holy. In Hebrew it is *Yira Shalem:* City or Legacy of Peace. Things haven't been peaceful in Jerusalem for a very long time. She is a city of contradictions and conflict.

We lost sight of the Dome as we came down the Mount of Olives into the busy streets lacing in the ancient walled city from the modern one. Crowds flowed in and out of the Damascus Gate as we drove past, traditional robes and modern dress compressed in the bottleneck to get through the stone arch, and then separating each to his own kind.

Our few days in Jerusalem were full of shopping and touring. We spent our shekels in the markets of the ancient walled city. We visited the Church of the Holy Sepulcher and the Garden Tomb. We ate kabobs and Arabic bread dipped in olive oil and spices.

Jerusalem's old stone corridors seemed to belong to us. The shopkeepers spoke English, and mild weather enticed us to explore the twists and turns of cobblestone lanes. The city's beauty deceived me; I was taken in for hours at a time by her skin-deep peace.

Then I would catch sight of an Israeli soldier with his gun slung over one shoulder and would remember where we were. It isn't so different, I thought—taken as I am by flights of fancy—not so different from when the Romans policed this place in the first century.

For Protestants—like me—who practice our faith in thought and memorial, a visit to Jerusalem fills a fleshly need to be connected to this earth. The physical becomes sacred. We touch what Jesus touched, walk where Jesus walked.

Over the three days we explored Jerusalem's ancient streets, our shoes became dusty with the land itself. When we returned to Jordan—then Jeanne to Nebraska, Scott and Michelle to Africa—we carried holy dust right along with us to the ends of the earth.

Michelle and I ducked into an Armenian Orthodox church to observe a midday service. I placed my open palm against the ancient stone walls. The oil from my hands left a part of me there. At an evangelical Christian bookstore I bought an olivewood dove for Laurie. Carrying that symbol of peace wrapped in tissue paper, I came out of the shop and stepped off the curb to avoid an Israeli soldier with machine gun ammunition draped across his chest, like the banner of a beauty queen.

Our last evening in Jerusalem, Todd and his mother stayed at the hostel with our girls while Scott walked with Michelle and me along cobblestone streets to the Wailing Wall. We had on light fleece jackets, but it was such a mild evening that we would have been comfortable in shirtsleeves. Inside Jerusalem's ancient walls, I felt alive and safe.

At the Wailing Wall we stood on the street above the sunken area where the devout come to pray—men on one side, women on the other. The wall was illuminated for evening, its stones glowing yellow in the artificial light. We could have been looking down at an ice rink from the second level of a shopping mall. Spread out along the ancient wall below, descendents of Moses and Abraham prayed side by side. They rocked at varying tempos, gliding deep into prayer. The women, separated from the men by a perpendicular dividing wall, seemed to favor prayer spots where they could almost tuck their covered heads into wide clefts in the rock.

The Wailing Wall is the only piece of the second temple left standing after the Romans tore it down in A.D. 70. The Jews who didn't escape the city before Rome surrounded it perished within her walls, embraced in death by her ancient stones. Some Christian traditions teach that when Jesus threw down tables and drove men out of the temple his action heralded her ultimate and complete destruction. Like the smashed tables, the temple walls would fall. Like the moneychangers, worshipers would be driven out of the temple—even God would withdraw his presence and leave the temple in ruins. Other Christians insist that the Jews will rise again to build yet another temple from the ground up.

Confident as each religious tradition might be, Jerusalem's future is unknown. Even her history is interpreted variously; it blurs, and none remember clearly.

In Mark's gospel and in Luke's, Jesus warned of coming destruction. In his words was an echo of the Babylonian army sacking Jerusalem centuries earlier—only this time destruction would come at the hand of Rome: *When you see Jerusalem surrounded by armies, then know that the desolation has come near.* Interpreted through the subsequent fall of the city in A.D. 70 it seems clear—Jesus prophesied that Jerusalem would be trampled underfoot by the Gentiles.

And she was. The holy city was brought to her knees, like a woman caught in adultery. Her walls were thrown down, her holy places exposed. The children who clung to her breast died in the ruins, while those who abandoned the holy city survived by escaping her walls and scattering to the four winds like seeds broadcast with no respect for property lines or borders, hurled far and wide, as if the farmer were intent upon claiming all lands as his own.

Scott, Michelle, and I stood at the Wailing Wall for a long time as if hypnotized by the worshipers bobbing and rocking at different tempos. The movement seemed to transport them deep into their prayers. One Hasidic man stood still in the midst of the waves of motion. The breeze lifted his side locks and threw them back over his shoulder. What thoughts came to him on that breeze, interrupting his prayers? What memories and hopes?

When the night air turned cool we walked back into the walled city to find our way through the stone corridors and back to the hostel.

We took a wrong turn at one point and ended up in the Arab quarter. A group of little boys, eight and nine-year-olds I guessed, Palestinian boys out in a Jewish neighborhood after curfew, were being herded home by two Israeli soldiers, each carrying an Uzi. The boys laughed as they pushed and bumped one another through the maze of stone corridors, the soldiers and their machine guns guiding from behind. One of the boys nudged his companion in a universal gesture that said: Dare me? He bent down to pick up a stone, and the back of my neck prickled.

Michelle grabbed my jacket and pulled me into a side doorway. The Arab kid tossed the stone against the ground ahead of him. It ricocheted off of a corner wall; then he picked it up off the ground and bounced it ahead once again.

Up ahead we saw a familiar market corridor that would lead us back to the Jaffa Gate and our hostel. As the boys and soldiers turned right we passed them on the left. I brushed against one of the guns and felt a tingle run up my spine. My shoe was untied; I bent over to tie it once the soldiers were well behind us. A soldier called out and the shoestring broke off in my hand. Was he yelling for me? I dropped the broken lace and hurried with Scott and Michelle toward the Jaffa Gate where Todd and the girls were safe behind stone walls. But, no. Jerusalem's masonry is neither solid nor safe. Her walls have fallen time and again throughout history. Safety and peace in Jerusalem are an illusion.

We left the next day. To avoid a roadblock near our hostel the taxi driver arranged to meet us all the way over at the Damascus Gate. We bumped our wheeled suitcases across the cobblestones, past Jewish shops, through the Christian quarter, and out into the Arab market near the Damascus Gate, where most of the shoppers and merchants are Muslim.

Our driver waited for us outside the walled city. He tied our suitcases up onto the roof of the extra-long taxi while we settled the children in the rear seat and climbed in after them, and then the driver handed the smaller bags in to us through the windows.

As we drove up the Mount of Olives, the golden rotunda of the Dome of the Rock grew smaller behind us, like a sun setting to the west, until Jerusalem was out of sight. Traveling across the desert and over the Jordan River, we headed out to the ends of the earth.

CHAPTER 20

FLEE TO
THE MOUNTAINS

Fires everywhere—and so much blood. The people trapped inside swarmed like panicked ants when the mound is disturbed.

But even in the swarm there was order, a plan. When the Roman army breached the gate, the Zealots, not afraid to kill, decided that death was better than rape. Suicide was preferable to torture and slavery and the Roman sword. First each man killed his own wife and children. In silence the fresh widowers drew lots. Those ten killed their hundreds of neighbors; each man lay down to die next to his slain family. At the end there was one man left living, the blood of his fellows warm and sticky under his feet as he fell on his own sword.

We cross the border from Jordan into Israel and drive for hours across the Judean Desert. Braxton Hicks contractions tighten my belly, and I shift sideways in my seat. The taxi we ride in is a long sedan with two full rows of passenger seats to accommodate the seven of us. Its interior smells of stale cigarette smoke and old leather and another odor I don't want to guess at. The driver puts in a cassette and sings along in Arabic while he hurtles us down the lonely desert highway. My toddler sleeps in my arms. No car seats and no seat belts. In the rear seat my four-year-old daughter sways cheerfully each time the road serpentines.

We pass Jericho and the open caves of Qumran. Ahead of us the plateaus surrounding Masada rise on the horizon. To their east the Dead Sea seems to siphon its intense blue color from the heavens until the pale sky gives up her brilliance to the salt sea. Masada rises from the Dead Sea Valley like an island in the sand. This flat-topped rock was home first to King Herod before the time of Christ, then home—and burial ground—to the Jewish Zealots one hundred years later, after the fall of Jerusalem in A.D. 70.

At the base of the fortress, palm trees outline the parking lot where Todd arranges for the driver to wait a couple of hours while we tour.

"Don't take the Snake Path," our driver calls out over his music as we walk toward the mountain.

We head to the cable car station to ride instead of hiking. Gondolas ascend and descend on cables that stretch above the winding trail. Some tourists still climb the Snake Path in the early morning before temperatures climb and heat exhaustion threatens. We're glad to crowd into the gondola for the aerial ride.

Closed in by adults, four-year-old Laurie has no view through the gondola windows. It's just as well that she can't look down and see how very high we are already, suspended above the Snake Path. The man standing in front of her wears the wire glasses and leather backpack of a European tourist. Each time he shifts to point out the view to his traveling companion his backpack pushes against the side of Laurie's face. For most of the close ride she puts her hands up over eyes and nose, creating her own private fortress.

The cable car docks and Laurie is pushed out ahead of us by the crowd. I duck between bodies to take her by the hand. Short as she is in the midst of the crowd, she can't see that we're still well below the summit. A boardwalk stretches along the side of the mountain all the way to a modern staircase. I'm pushed along with my daughter, a crowd before and behind us. I have her walk next to the mountain face to keep her away from the parapet view of the steep drop.

She is flushed and red from climbing these stairs, but I can't carry her. Todd, just ahead of me, has fifteen-month old Ashley in his arms, and I'm five months pregnant. Laurie begs for a rest but we can't step aside on this narrow stairway. With people pushing up from behind there is no way to turn around and go back. I tell her to press on, that it will soon be over.

When we reach the top she sits right in the dust and whines that her tummy hurts, her legs too. I'm embarrassed that other tourists stare at her. She's a sweet-natured child and doesn't make scenes like this; it makes me wonder what's really wrong with her. It must just be the hours of driving across the desert without a stop and then this climb up several flights on a warm day.

"Seems like a rest would help," I tell Todd. "I'll stay here with her, where it's shady. Go on and catch up with the others."

When I was Laurie's age, traveling in the back seat for long hours and waiting for my father to read every word of every historical marker, I found a secret way to pass the time. I pretended to be from the past, drawn out of time and place and plopped down in the twentieth century in the form of a pale-skinned little girl riding at frightening speeds in the back seat of some horseless carriage. Following my parents down trails or gazing out over canyon vistas, my game of pretend gave me new eyes to see my own adventures. I traveled through Colorado as a Native American, through Utah as a pioneer, and across the long desert roads of Nevada and California as a Bible character.

"Pretend you're one of the little Jewish girls who lived here," I say.

"Don't want to. My head hurts."

"Come on, sweetie, it's fun to pretend."

"Can the little girl have a pet?"

I tell her that a Zealot girl would surely have made friends with the wild creatures, just like Dickon did in *The Secret Garden*.

"With birds?"

"Sure, with birds."

She peers into the bright sky, but the sparrows aren't flying this high.

"Mama, my head hurts too much—and my side."

Even in the shade it's so warm. The Braxton-Hicks contractions return and I wish I'd thought to bring a bottle of water.

At the time of the Zealots' mass suicide, in A.D. 73 or 74, there was water here, and food, too—plenty of it. That's why they were able to stick it out so long, why Rome couldn't starve them out.

Herod the Great built Masada before the birth of Christ. He had massive cisterns created in two levels. Channels cut through the rock diverted the runoff from surrounding mountains, transforming dry earth and rock into a paradise of Roman baths and running water. While the Jews in Palestine sent their women to draw water from wells, Herod, king of the Jews, luxuriated with the uncircumcised Romans in hot baths and steam.

Herod was no Messiah, prostrating himself to Rome as he did. He ruled the Jews because Rome ruled and had given him a tiny corner of Palestine to watch over. He ate unclean foods and skipped out on holy days. He had no love for the house of David. His Jewish subjects called him Herod the Impious.

Herod built his fortress at Masada as a pleasure palace, but it also was an elaborate security measure for the unpopular ruler, fearful as he was of revolt or conquest. Herod had plenty of enemies. Within his own kingdom were Jews known as Zealots, their eyes ever on the horizon watching for Messiah, that king of the Jews who would lead them in battle. The Zealots yearned to rise up and judge Rome and the servants of Rome, to overthrow the enemy and take back Jerusalem. They knew that judgment was near, that great Day of the Lord when the blood of the faithless would run through the streets. The true Messiah would overthrow the Gentile usurpers by force. There was no room for peace.

Many times during Herod's reign there were small uprisings among the Zealots, rumors of Messiah. Herod, wielding the power of Rome, suppressed every hint of unrest—even so much as the whisper of a baby boy born at census time, infant king of the Jews.

Around the time of the birth of Christ, Masada became a Roman outpost and was home to a small garrison of soldiers from A.D. 6 to A.D. 66. After Herod's death Rome continued to rule Palestine through prefects and proconsuls. Herod's sons bowed to Rome as their father had, including Herod Antipas, tetrarch of Galilee and the east bank of the Jordan. Year after year the Zealots resisted Rome in their hearts while they watched and waited to revolt.

Some of the Zealot insurgents carried small daggers, called *sicae,* under their cloaks. The *Sicarii* could quickly thrust and dash before marketplace crowds noticed the fallen man. Almost always the dead man was a Jew sympathetic to Rome. Finally their hour came in A.D. 66, less than a generation after the death of Christ. The Roman procurator in Jerusalem stole cartloads of silver from the holy temple. Messiah or no Messiah, the Zealots took up daggers and swords, even stones, and they revolted, slaughtering the Roman troops stationed at Jerusalem and taking back the holy city after decades of Roman occupation. Far to Jerusalem's south, Sicarii Zealots led by Elazar ben Yair seized Masada from the Roman garrison stationed there. By the time Roman armies surrounded Jerusalem's walls in A.D. 70, several hundred Jews had fled to Masada and were sheltered there. Those left in Jerusalem found no escape. Once Rome breached the walls of the holy city, all inside perished.

She's more insistent about this pain in her side, and I'm starting to think she won't settle out of it, that something is really wrong. Or should I discipline her? I know every mother of a bratty kid would say this when they're embarrassed about their child's behavior in public, but it's not like her to act this way.

Passing tourists turn and stare. They must think I'm abusing her by not offering comfort, or worse that I did something to make her cry like this. A mother should know what to do. I feel as if I'm not her mother at all. I don't know what she needs. I read the markers and try to translate them into a four-year-old's history lesson to distract her. But the story of Masada is not a comforting one.

At the base of Masada, the outlines of eight camps set around the siege wall are now lines traced in the dust, as if a god pulled his finger through the sand, spelling out judgment.

The desert highway sidewinds north, and a lone car on it looks as small as a snake's eye. This morning's tourists must have seen us coming for kilometers, just as the Zealots saw Rome's Tenth Legion advancing toward them. Masada was the last Zealot outpost. Those who fled Jerusalem while there was still time were welcomed at Masada. At news of Jerusalem's destruction by the Romans in A.D. 70, Masada's Zealots wept to hear that the great Temple lay in ruins, not one stone left upon another.

Behind me are the crumbled walls of Herod's storerooms where the Sicarii Zealots found larder to keep them from starving. That's one way that history tells it. Another version has them raiding surrounding communities, terrorizing other Jews, stealing food and carting it back to stock the Masada storehouses.

Two thousand years of rain and sun have cast their own judgment on this place: slowly the stones have fallen; slowly the masonry has come apart. From a god's-eye view these ruins would look like crumbs off a broken loaf.

There were survivors. Two women and five children hid in a cistern during the mass suicide. Because they lived to tell Josephus, the first-century historian, we have an account of what went on that night.

The Roman soldiers encamped at the base of Masada for over a year, unable to find a way into Herod's fortress. The only way in would be from above, but the gods did not cast judgment directly from the heavens. Over months the Romans built up a long ramp from the desert floor to the top of the cliff wall and the base of Masada's fortress, to give access for their battering rams and catapults. That ramp still stands as testament and hundreds of cannonball-sized stones still lie within Masada's crumbling walls. With the enemy now just outside the gate, the only defense left to the Zealots was to heave boulders onto their attackers. To drive the Zealots back from the wall, the Romans set fire to the wall's wooden reinforcements and the desert wind turned the flames into angry pillars of smoke and fire.

Elazar ben Yair rallied the Zealots to their final act of defiance against Rome: "Let our wives die before they are abused, and our children before they have tasted of slavery, and after we have slain them, let us bestow that glorious benefit upon one another mutually."

Laurie's cries are louder now and high pitched. She's holding her side. Is the appendix on the left or right? She looks feverish. I reach out to put my hand against her flushed cheek, and she pushes me away, screams.

"Don't Mama, don't touch me. It hurts, Mama."

We're surrounded by ruins and hot sky and dust. So isolated. There must be a hospital in Jerusalem, doctors—but we're hours away. This place is an open-air crypt.

I think of the Zealot woman, the survivor, in the year leading up to that night of smoke and fire and blood. She watched Rome's progress as weeks became months and the enemy's siege wall stood six feet deep all around the base of Masada. Every day the Zealots ate and drank from Herod's storehouses and cisterns. Did they count provisions to see how long they could hold out against Rome? Perhaps they already realized that their storehouses would outlast the strength of Masada's walls.

With the enemy surrounding and thick smoke biting her eyes the woman must have known that the desolation was near. Mothers were perhaps the most cursed, the hands that nursed and comforted now pressed over the children's mouths to silence their cries. According to Josephus, the Zealots saw the fall of Masada as judgment from their own god. The men decided it. All would die together, their own hands carrying out the divine will.

But that woman didn't lay down her life. I see her as if she yet lives. I imagine that when her husband takes the baby's body to lay it with its bloody siblings, she slips out. In the dark, another mother and her frightened children huddle against a wall. One child, a girl, cries out.

"Don't touch me," she screams.

She's bent knees to chest and won't let me hold her. Where is Todd? Can't he hear her across the ruins? Why doesn't he come? The European tourist stares. He takes a step toward us and I look away—to discourage him if possible. I don't need advice or accusations now.

Against the side of a stone wall I see an abandoned pack. Whose is it? When my daughter takes a breath between screams I think I hear it ticking. We have to get away but where can we hide? How can I get her to come with me?

The owner of the pack comes from behind a stone wall, gives me a grin, makes a comment I can't hear over my child's cries. I don't think to ask him for water or for help.

Todd returns, and it's so simple. We're not trapped in history or in a pact of self-destruction. No army surrounds us. Someone brings a bottle of water and our daughter calms as she drinks from it.

We leave because we can. On our cable car descent we hang by a slender thread over the desert abyss. The Dead Sea looks refreshing in the afternoon light. It glitters and deceives; I know that the Dead Sea does not refresh. Its salty shoreline is the lowest dry land on earth. Water enters through only one source, the Jordan River. Since rivers don't flow uphill, water spills into the Dead Sea and never leaves. There's no circulation. No way out.

The palm trees outlining the parking lot appear to grow in size as we descend until we touch down near the oasis of tourist shopping, museum, and restaurant.

More water, rest, and a meal on the restaurant's shady veranda restore Laurie's usual peace. A vestigial sadness reminds me that there was no escape for the Zealots whose bones long ago turned to dust. Here their future died. Here they surrendered hope, their unborn dying with them.

In the gift shop display window, bottles of Dead Sea salts beckon in unnatural colors: cobalt blue, banana yellow, red. Would the dye from the salts turn my bath water yellow? Or red like the blood that flowed here on the day of slaughter? My own unborn child kicks my rib.

What about the two women along with the five children who hid from death—did they live out their lives in slavery, in shame? I don't know how they lived, only that they did. Perhaps they heard the echo of Jesus' words, spoken to their parents and grandparents in Roman-occupied Palestine: *When you see Jerusalem surrounded by armies, then know that its desolation is near. Let those who are in Judea flee to the mountains.*

In the belly of the mountain, those seven were saved.

My daughter is her four-year-old self again. She finds her way between tables to where small birds cock their heads sideways to watch the foreign child approach. A breeze lifts and tousles her hair as she sips fresh water and throws breadcrumbs to the sparrows.

CHAPTER 21

ARABIAN NIGHTS

"Hey, Mom—doesn't that look like Arabic writing on the road?"

Laurie asks about the long, wavering strips of dark tar along the asphalt. We drive this freeway every day in and out of Fort Worth, where my girls now attend the classical school where Todd is headmaster. There they learn Latin, not Arabic.

"Maybe one of the road workers was an Arab, Mom. He got bored at work and wrote a story all along the freeway. Do you think?" The tar does look like some mysterious script. A thousand and one Arabian miles. The tar line squiggles and blurs. I enter into Laurie's imaginative thought of stories written lengthwise down the roads we travel.

"Mom, do you think I could still speak Arabic—if I went back to Jordan?"

"I don't know for sure, honey."

Laurie remembers Jordan in snippets. But she doesn't remember any Arabic. Sometimes she'll ask me to teach her, and for a few days we'll rehearse greetings. Latin comes to her more easily nowadays.

One day when I picked Laurie up from the Arabic pre-school her teacher beamed with pride. We'd been living in Jordan seven months.

"Laurie speaks in perfect Arabic today," she told me. "A jet flew over and she said that the *big airplane is up* and then she asked me to *tell the airplane to go faster, O Teacher!*"

Todd and I spent mornings in Arabic classes and afternoons studying, yet here our daughter played in the sandbox and spoke Arabic as an afterthought.

On our bus rides home from language school Laurie climbed off my lap and reached her arms out to be lifted up into a stranger's arms. In Jordan, children are protected and loved by all and are raised to trust adults. Everyone is "auntie" or "uncle" to a Jordanian child. Laurie took candy from stranger after stranger as is the Arab custom—children are honored by the entire community, and our daughter was treated as well as any firstborn Arab son. I resisted my American impulse to teach her to be suspicious and guarded with strangers, resisted my urge to inspect the candy before she ate it. We were the parents, but in cultural adjustment we followed our daughter's lead.

Amman is a city of hills and its residents never simply "go" anywhere. We learned the Arabic for, "I'm ascending to the market," or "I'm descending to my home." The geography of Amman's dialect requires sloping travel verbs. As Amman grows outward, suburbs spread to induct new hills into the city; now it reaches across more than twenty hills in that bumpy landscape. Our first neighborhood lowered itself down the backside of one of the original seven hills, *Ashrafiya,* then spread to form a shopping district in the brief valley before apartment buildings and villas climbed other, smaller hills outside of town.

Directly across the lane from our apartment stood an undeveloped expanse of land where shepherds led mixed flocks of shaggy sheep and goats to graze. In spring, women and children picnicked there. I went down to join them, handing Laurie over to an older girl to be entertained while I spoke fledgling Arabic with a delighted neighbor.

We moved closer to language school, to the apartment with the wraparound balcony. We finished our year at the language institute, and Todd went on to study Arabic at Jordan University while I worked with a language helper at home. Laurie continued to go to preschool each morning, playing with her friend Yezzin and speaking "perfect" Arabic to her teachers and classmates.

We finished our Arabic studies and Todd found work in Amman and signed a two-year contract. Student visas were changed to residency cards. We moved to the large, ground-floor flat in the Jalal family's building. Ashley was born a month later.

At six months old Ashley grew ill. Refused her baby food. Lying on a flannel receiving blanket on the floor, she slept five hours at a time—more if I didn't wake her to nurse. She even slept through the diaper changes. When I held the diaper up to examine the contents, I saw what seemed like streaks of worms or blood. Our pediatrician answered my page from the hospital. "I'm sure she's fine," he said to my description of symptoms. "I'll be doing rounds a little longer. If it will make you feel better meet me before twenty minutes' time."

At the hospital emergency room Ashley seemed to perk up. She looked at the pediatrician and smiled.

"See? It's nothing," he said to me.

I wanted him to be right. Probably what looked like blood in her diaper was some bit of undigested food—

except she hadn't had anything but breast milk for days. And what if he was wrong?

"You're still worried," the pediatrician said. "We will send a stool sample for your sake."

Two days later I hadn't heard from the doctor or the lab. I was growing accustomed to Ashley's listless sleep. I got things done while she slept hours and hours. She didn't cry. She wasn't in pain.

Our friend Mark came over. Mark was a Fulbright scholar—a doctor himself, working in infectious diseases. "This baby should not be acting like this," he told me. "Something is very wrong."

"They would have called me if they found something in her stool, right?"

"That's the thing," Mark said. His intensity scared me. "The system here doesn't work like ours." Mark knew a Jordanian patient who died just days before of a common bacterial infection, while under a doctor's care. The doctor prescribed an antibiotic and drew blood for the lab. Test results showed that the antibiotic she was taking would not kill the infection she had, but her doctor never called the lab to check. The Jordanian lab technicians didn't call her doctor. The ill woman's lab results sat neatly filed as she died of an infection that could easily have been treated.

"You have to be your own advocate here," Mark said. "Don't wait. She's very ill. Promise me, Lisa. Promise you'll call today."

So I called the lab. Salmonella. Then I called the pediatrician and told him the lab results myself. He prescribed the right antibiotic and Ashley took it. She recovered. I don't let myself think of what might have happened if Mark hadn't been there, so much more concerned about my daughter than I was.

I found a new pediatrician who was herself the mother of young children. When Ashley, at twenty months, yanked against Todd's grasp in a parking lot and dislocated her elbow, our new pediatrician pulled and rotated it back into position. She called me at home the next morning. "I couldn't sleep," she said. "I was worried about little Ashley. How is her arm this morning?"

When my third daughter was born, this was the pediatrician who laughed at my jingle bells on the door and consented to let baby Jessica stay with me instead of in the hospital nursery. She loved my children, and I loved her for it.

When we left Jordan I made a special visit to her clinic to say goodbye, with tears in my eyes. I have never found a doctor like her again. I miss her.

Our home was always dusty. Twice weekly mopping kept it under control and we gave the girls baths most nights. Sometimes we started the process right after dinner—way too early, but they couldn't read the clock and didn't realize. We skipped brushing teeth on those nights and still the girls didn't catch on that something was different. Todd read a bedtime story to the two older girls while I nursed the baby. We tucked them all in, knowing it would change in a minute or two, savoring the suspense.

Todd turned out the bedroom light and took two steps out into the hall—then, "Surprise! *Pajama Ride!*"

The girls sat up wide-eyed, then joyful and incredulous when they realized how we'd fooled them yet again. They laughed at wearing shoes with nightgowns. We gave piggyback rides out to the car and drove through the freshly darked streets of Amman to the ice cream parlor, where young Arab men who dipped out our ice cream chuckled at children in pajamas eating ice cream. *Those strange Americans again.*

Laurie chose mint chip. Ashley got a plain sugar cone without ice cream and went to work on it with her brand new teeth. Baby Jessica slept in her car seat, nestled at my feet. Our girls didn't have a lot of things that children in America had—but we tried to make life in Jordan special for them.

Before Laurie started kindergarten, we returned to the U.S. for good. In our first months back we had pajama rides a couple of times. It wasn't the same. No warm desert breeze through the car windows, no amused Arabs watching us and grinning. Pajama rides are now among the girls' magic-carpet memories of those good years in Jordan.

"Tell us about pajama rides, Mom!"

I am the storyteller, resurrecting family memory for even the daughters who weren't born yet when we lived in that pie-wedge apartment. I build our mythology through pasting photographs in large albums and speaking shared memories into my children's hearts. The chapters of our life in the Middle East have become our family lore. These are the tales we tell and retell to root ourselves. We are Harrises. Once upon a time, we lived in the Middle East.

A voice from the back seat pulls me into the present as we exit the Fort Worth freeway. It's Jessica, who is now eight years old.

"Mom, I was born in Jordan, right?"

"Yes, you were born in Jordan, honey."

"Tell me a story about it, Mom. Please. Just one story."

So I will tell her a story—a true story—about our life in Jordan.

CHAPTER 22

Finding Nadia

In the wee hours of morning when I ought to be writing I do an Internet search once again for my childhood pen pal, Nadia. A new listing shows up in the search results—but it's old information. Nadia's name is listed among the contributors to a small, out-of-print literary magazine. Is this *my* Nadia? She's a *writer?* Why hasn't this information come up on any of my other periodic Internet searches for Nadia?

I shoot an email off to the editor. It's a long shot. He's probably not even checking this old email address. The magazine has been out of print for years. This Nadia is probably another woman. What are the chances?

By the end of the day the editor writes back. Nadia is a physician of East Indian descent, living in Saudi Arabia. She's the same Nadia. She's a friend of the editor's. When he published his wife's essay about cooking chicken masala with Nadia he included Nadia's name and recipe. He'll forward my email on to Nadia, and he's glad to be of help. Would I like to read an essay he wrote about visiting Nadia in Saudi Arabia several months ago? I would. His words paint Nadia's life for me. She's married and has children. Her life is good.

Over the next few days I check my email more frequently than usual. Nadia was a huge part of my childhood and adolescence, but was I the same quality of friend for her that she was for me? I know she had other pen pals. For Nadia, I was one of many. I hope she remembers me.

The message is waiting for me one morning when I rise at 4:00 a.m. to write.

Lisa,
I cannot believe this! I am so excited to hear from you, Lisa. Please update me on your life. I have to work now but quickly I'll say that I'm married with two kids. A boy, 12 and a girl, 10. I work at a hospital as a family physician part time. My husband works for ARAMCO.

This is wonderful!
Nadia

Our correspondence is renewed with long emails from me and brief but warm responses from the busy doctor-mom in Saudi. I don't mind. I'm thrilled to have my old friend back and will receive gladly whatever part of herself she offers.

Nadia sends pictures. Her daughter's name is Ruby. I can't believe it. Like the genus *Rubus,* like the ruby raspberries Nadia and I shared at the edge of an Oregon wood. This little girl shines like the gem that shares her name. Eyebrows arch over her wide and bright brown eyes. A pink bow holds back Ruby's curls. She is Nadia's child, and in her I see my childhood friend.

When my family moved to Oregon just before my sixteenth birthday, I started life over. The California friends I'd grown up with finished high school without me. I graduated from high school in Oregon and went on to college with a few of my classmates. Twenty years later I'm still in touch with some of them. When they email pictures of their children, I see brand-new faces. Nadia is the only friend left in my life who knew me before I was a teenager—who knew me when we were both Ruby's age.

This friendship was established through correspondence on onionskin paper, across time zones and continents. In my letters to Nadia, I used to call her "my Saudi sister." She is still exactly that.

We don't exchange emails often. Nadia is busy, and that's fine. She's there if I need her like any best friend, like a sister. I know how to find her, and I hear from her when there's news.

"This is so nice," she wrote in one email.

And it is.

CHAPTER 23

TANGLED HOUSEHOLDS

My four daughters sprawl on the family room floor with two large photo albums spread open before them. Their grandmother comes out from her in-law suite and takes her place on the couch. I tell the stories again, and we remember.

Pictures in the album show fifteen-month-old Laurie with her cheeks ruddy from the cold, looking out the window of our first home in Jordan. Below her in the rocky field neighbor ladies stand conversing while sheep and goats follow their shepherd up from the road and into the field.

Turn the album page and blond Laurie sits at a table crowded with Arab preschoolers. She is youngest and smallest. Pages later she poses between newborn twins. A close up shot shows the ash smears on the forehead of each infant.

Laurie and Yezzin crawl behind furniture. They lie on the cool tile balcony and lean heads back to look at the camera. Laurie laughs at this lovely desert life.

On a plush blue sofa in the flat we rented from the Jalal family Laurie looks suddenly tall and grown up as she reaches a gentle hand out to caress her newborn sister. As the album pages are turned baby Ashley lifts her head, sits up without support, and crawls over tile floors. Her knees and the tops of her feet are dark with dust. She stands up to walk and reaches out her own tiny hand to greet another baby sister born in Jordan when Ashley was nineteen months old.

These albums chronicle our years in Jordan. Organizing them was easy. I simply affixed images on the timeline of births and children growing up.

I haven't put my pictures from Damascus in an album—precious as they are to me. The snapshots are in all different sizes, some from the cameras of classmates and some taken by my Syrian friends. The colors of the ones processed in Syria have already faded. These snapshots, taken years before marriage and children, are harder to place on a timeline. Harder to categorize. I examine them closely for details, for what I may have missed. Looking at them, I have the same out-of-body feeling I had as a young woman, when I would meet my own eyes in the mirror and ask, "Who am I? Why am I here?"

Who was I in Damascus? Who shall I yet become?

Served cold in tall glasses our hibiscus tea gleamed vermilion in the sun.

"This is what Egyptians drink," Mona explained, "but we like it here in Damascus, too."

Mona and I sipped the sweet-tangy tea and tasted memories not our own: the Nile's slow rolling under the African sun; the layered limestone in the Valley of the Kings; hibiscus growing wild in the Nile Valley; dried petals of cranberry red heaped in baskets at the spice market in Old Cairo.

On the other side of the sunny courtyard Yasmine worked. She dipped her bucket in the fountain and dumped water out on the tiles. Then with a small broom she scrubbed the courtyard and swept the dirty water toward the drain at the base of the fountain. Yasmine was married to Mona's brother. I could have believed she was the maid and not a family member at all.

Two toddlers played in the puddled water. The little girls were Mona's nieces, one her sister's child and the other her brother and Yasmine's, all of them living together in this eleven-room home in the Old City of Damascus. The chunky toddler pressed her hand into a puddle and painted wet handprints on the dry portion of tile. Her skinny cousin picked at the beads around her ankle, perhaps a charm to help her gain weight, perhaps a talisman against the evil eye.

I felt like the proverbial fly on the wall: a watcher. Mona was a student at Damascus University, and the day we met she invited me home. As we drank the hibiscus tea, Mona chatted to me about her studies, her hopes for marriage . . . the words softened and blurred to a murmur the way background noises fade and disappear as dreams take over the mind. Absorbed with watching the family, I tuned in to Mona's buzzing chatter only when she told me something about her mysterious family. So much was veiled in this household and I wanted to understand it all.

Mona's brother entered the courtyard and the women hurried to bring him lunch. Even while he kissed his mother and thanked her for the meal his eyes were on Yasmine. She continued to work while her husband ate, smiling at him with lively eyes as she swept and scrubbed. From time to time her mother-in-law would call out an order, and Yasmine would immediately comply.

I couldn't help noticing how much more beautiful Yasmine was than her sisters- or mother-in-law. And because I grew up reading fairy tales I couldn't help assuming that they were jealous of her beauty.

In the Cinderella story from *The Arabian Nights*[†] a genie from an alabaster pot replaces the fairy godmother and glass slippers become a gold anklet. Surely Yasmine was formed by her Arabian fairy tale just as I was by the Cinderella from my own storybook.

As a girl I thought my mother required too many chores of me—too much dishwashing and vacuuming and dusting. My family often burned logs in the fireplace on cool nights, but my mother cleaned out the ashes herself. The irony, of course, escaped me.

At eighteen, with no Prince Charming on the horizon, I moved out. When I returned for visits I did not bring laundry home like the rest of my college friends did. There was plenty of work for me to do at my parents' house without adding extra laundry to the list. If dirty dishes had piled up in my mother's kitchen, I soaked and scrubbed them. In my mother's home I couldn't rest. It had always been my role to do the household chores.

The Cinderella Complex is described by psychotherapist Colette Dowling as a woman's unconscious desire to be taken care of by others. In my case the complex reversed itself. My conscious identification with the Cinderella story compelled me to take care of others, to do any work that needed doing. Eventually, it made me seek independence—

[†]Geraldine McCaughrean, "The Anklet," *One Thousand and One Arabian Nights* (Oxford: Oxford University Press, 1999).

not Prince Charming. I moved out of my parents' home when I was eighteen. I didn't marry Todd until I was twenty-seven. Three years later we had Laurie. After we moved to the Middle East Ashley was born, and I became pregnant with Jessica.

Then Todd's father died. Jeanne, widowed in Nebraska, was isolated from her sons—one in Africa, one in Hawaii, and one in the Middle East. When Todd and I returned to the U.S. she'd been widowed less than a year. I convinced her, over time, that it would be best for her to live closer to us. We've shared a household for seven years.

A memory stands propped in my mind like an old snapshot. It is the day my mother-in-law moved in with us. We are all smiling and relaxed. No more financial worries for my husband and me. No more loneliness for Jeanne. No more long trips so the girls can see their grandmother. That snapshot moment is like the last page of a fairy tale, and we're about to live happily ever after.

Only we haven't.

I think of Yasmine often these days. She seemed to be full of joy, even living with her mother-in-law. There must be some nugget of wisdom for me if I dig hard enough into the past. If I can understand Yasmine perhaps I will understand myself. Perhaps I can find contentment.

Squeeze the past like a sponge,
Smell the present like a rose,
And send a kiss to the future.
—Arabic proverb

I have two photos taken in Yasmine's courtyard one sunny Damascus day. In the first my university friend Mona stands in front of the heptagonal fountain. A single stream of water rises from the fountain as if from a broken lawn sprinkler. Planted in rusty cans around the rim of the fountain grow many rootings and rerootings of the same plant. From one of the six plants three blossoms rise. Mona is alone in the picture but I know that Yasmine stands off camera holding her broom.

In the second photo the toddlers sit on the edge of the fountain, bare feet dangling. The thin toddler wearing blue and white beads around her ankle is uncomfortable; perhaps the stonework is cold against her bare legs. Yasmine's daughter sits beside her, chunky and serene. Like her mother, the child wears no gold and no talismans.

Mona worried about her sister's thin child. No matter what they did, she remained nervous and unhappy. She woke up screaming in the night. Surely she was too young to understand. What was the source of the nightmares?

"My sister divorced," Mona said. I had wondered about the sister. A narrow-faced young woman, she hardly looked old enough to be a bride let alone a mother and a divorcee.

"Her husband took a second wife," Mona explained. "He was a Saudi and they don't treat their women as well as Syrian men do. My sister has gold and she has her daughter, thanks be to Allah. Perhaps she will marry again." And then, leaning close, "It will not be easy for her to find a man who will marry her now."

During my Damascus days I journaled about these babies, how they haunted me. I tried to find meaning. I imagined that the thin child represented her narrow-faced mother's broken marriage and the chubby one represented the healthy love between Yasmine and her husband. In this photo the child I remember as thin does not appear sickly.

Comparing them arm for arm and ankle for ankle they both look perfectly healthy. Yasmine's daughter bears her mother's countenance. But in the thin child's eyes I see that she is not content. In the thin child's eyes I see myself.

On our mortgage note, there were only two signature lines. Jeanne signed first then passed the forms to Todd. When my turn came the loan officer showed me how to squeeze my name in next to Todd's in the white space of the form's margin. Legally speaking we are three homeowners with equal shares, but the times I've needed to discuss the mortgage with the bank I've had to explain who I am. The computerized version of the loan records, like the papers we signed, has but two fields for owners' names so on the screen only Todd and his mother appear to own our house.

When explaining her living situation Jeanne always says, "We share a home," implying that we are equal. One day when I was out running errands she answered the phone. The caller asked for the lady of the house. "Which one?" Jeanne asked, stumping the telemarketer, who had no scripted response. She repeated it to me with a chuckle when I got home.

There's no script for us, either. Who is the lady of our house?

The narrow-faced sister sat in a kitchen chair while Yasmine combed through her hair. She yelped with nearly every stroke of the comb, and Yasmine took smaller sections of hair to work out the knots more gently. The sister finally grabbed the comb away from Yasmine and threw it down. She spoke to Yasmine in a low voice and stomped up the stairs to the second floor. Yasmine's curls fell over her shoulder as she picked up the comb and swept stray hairs off the floor, pushing the kitchen chair softly back to its place.

The first November after we signed the mortgage Jeanne came home from the store one day with the trunk of her car full of canned yams, peas, and other holiday foods to be smothered in the gravies and cream sauces of a Southern menu. I understood without asking that, as the matriarch of the family, Thanksgiving dinner would be prepared according to her menu, not mine. I wish I could say it doesn't matter—that I'm content to fit into these long strands of family customs. But I strain against it. I want to cook from scratch instead of from a can, and I want to establish our own family's traditions the same way. Someday we will. Not yet, though.

We eat off Jeanne's pink lacy china every holiday—so different from the chunky, unmatched stoneware I favor. She likes me to set the table with her sterling—but it drives me nuts to polish it. And the silver flavors the food—or perhaps I taste gritty leftovers from my half-hearted polishing. Most years I hurry and set the table with stainless before she mentions the sterling. If she notices, she doesn't say anything.

Now she's frail and can't cook. When holidays come I shop according to the list in her shaky handwriting. She sits at the kitchen table and reads out her recipes, and I put together her smothered favorites. "Double—no triple this recipe," she says. No one will eat the extra. A week after the holiday I will dump the uneaten leftovers down the kitchen disposal.

I am her hands stirring the "glorified peas" and dumping them into an oiled casserole dish, crunching greasy potato chips over the top to form the crispy crust she loves. I am her arms lifting the pan of cornbread batter into the hot oven. She sits at the table as I open cans and melt extra sticks of butter. We cook for her dead husband and for sons too many miles away to share the meal. As the familiar smells fill the kitchen she remembers when she, too, was young and strong. When, in a household of boys and men, she was the undisputed lady of the house.

Jeanne reminisces about her sons and their childhood friends back on Old Oak Drive. How the Hoffer twins called her "Mom" and always managed to drop by the day she made her Christmas peanut butter fudge. Though my hands lift and stir, Jeanne is the one still cooking for a husband and three growing boys with their neighborhood pals dropping by.

What holiday traditions will my girls carry into their own homes when they leave ours?

Todd's brother Jeff, the psychologist, tells me that my discontent in sharing a household with his mother may well be unresolved issues from my Cinderella childhood. He's very kind to me and keeps his counselor's nudgings gentle. He has a PhD and has published two textbooks in his field, but we've read all the same fairy tales.

Growing up I don't think I felt rivalry with my mother like I do now with Jeanne. The roles were clear back then. Mom was the boss. I obeyed her. Memory paints me as a compliant child with strict parents. My mother doesn't remember my childhood the same way I do. She remembers me stomping my foot. Resisting her authority. In fact, the way she remembers it, I was a rebel even as a newborn.

Battling postpartum depression, my mother tried to breastfeed me. I spat out her breast and refused to take anything but formula. She says I didn't snuggle into her like my brothers after me—I drank my formula with my face turned out, neck stretched to see the world beyond my mother's embrace.

I pulled up to standing position at six months and walked at seven. My pediatrician called me "a little girl in a hurry."

On my first day of kindergarten my mother walked me to school, pushing my baby brother in a carriage. Two blocks from the school I told her to stop, that I would go the rest of the way myself.

My class photos from elementary school show a dreamy girl gazing at the camera with an absentminded half-smile. I got good grades and rarely had my name on the board. But was I really such a compliant child? What then are these snatches of memory? Staying in from recess while the other children shouted and played. Hiding humiliation with bravado when I had to safety pin the long yarn "tattle tail" to the seat of my pants. Clenching back tears when my favorite teacher took me aside—he wanted to give me the prize for best student, he said, but best student includes sitting still during assembly, and I hadn't.

Do I know my long-ago self at all? I study my school pictures as if the child I was might speak to the woman I am. The young me is mystery, and all I can touch and see of her are these frozen smiles, that one split second when the shutter clicked. Try as I might I can't conjure my thoughts from that day or week, let alone that one moment. Was I thinking of mischief? Of retaliation next recess? This I know: I was not a sweet Cinderella.

Any flesh-and-blood Prince Charming will get it wrong at some point. He'll stomp on his dance partner's toe. The glass shoe will slip from his klutzy fingers and crash to the ground. Cinderella will sass her stepmother. In real life the one-dimensional characters of childhood fairy tales become tangled with threads of hurt and good intentions, of jealousy, love, and self-protection.

Was Yasmine as content as I remember? Or have I made her into a fairy tale character too? Surely she lived under household tensions far greater than I know. I dig in the past; I unearth memories of the Arab family that so intrigued me. I take down the old photos and I look for clues. I hope to find some universal wisdom and press it down deep where it can change me. I need more than fairy tales.

Five years ago Jeanne fell and badly injured her left shoulder. She still can't lift her arm well enough to blow dry or curl her own hair. I style her hair on Sunday mornings so that it will look fresh and full for church. She never complains though I work through knots and sometimes without realizing hold the hot blow dryer too close to her scalp.

On her right earlobe two long hairs grow out of a mole, so I trim them. In her scalp near the hairline is a pimply looking cyst. I check it for changes and brush lightly over that section. When I first started fixing her hair the moles and hairs and cyst repelled me—like the way I felt about messy diapers and spit-up before I had a baby of my own.

You get used to these things.

The cyst hasn't changed but her hair is thinning. Some days it comes out in big chunks, and I have to turn off the dryer and clean the brush halfway through. As I see more of her skull through thinning skin, as death sneaks closer to the surface, I see life, too. I see my husband's features in hers.

Laurie has the same facial structure as her father and grandmother, framed by long, blond hair that reaches past her waist. When I remind her to brush it, she pulls the brush loosely over the top layer, leaving the tangles underneath. I comb it out for her a couple of times a week, all the way down to the roots, while she begs me to be gentler. I try to be slow and careful but it takes a certain amount of discomfort to untangle the knots. I lack patience.

"What's the point?" Laurie asks. "It's just going to get all messy again."

I don't have a good answer.

One doorway off of Yasmine's courtyard led to a small room beside the kitchen. There her father-in-law lay on a pallet, his wiry limbs drawn up tight and bent close to his body. He had a long gray beard like the respected Muslim men of the community who had been on the Hajj. Saliva wet his beard and dribbled in long strings to the pallet. As Yasmine rolled the dying man's thin body to one side and refolded the cloth that absorbed his drool did she see her young husband's features beneath the long beard and sagging skin?

Yasmine moved around to sit at the head of the pallet, lifting her father-in-law's head and shoulders and leaning him against her own chest. She dipped a spoon into a bowl of rice mashed in chicken broth—an Arab baby's first food. He took a few bites before turning his head away from the spoon. Yasmine lowered his head and shoulders back to the pallet. She bent low and gently kissed the old man's hairline.

Death is a black camel, says the Arabic proverb, *kneeling at everyone's door in turn.*

She says it's not a premonition and that I shouldn't make too much of it, but last week Jeanne asked me to sit down with her. She showed me where she keeps the information on the family plot and how she'd marked her address book so I would know who to call first. Cremation, no embalming. Instead of flowers, a memorial fund. Doesn't matter which hymns, just so they're ones that everyone knows.

There is less competition now for the role of lady of the house. Something is different, especially during the quiet hours of the day when the children are off at school. Almost peaceful.

There are tangles between us that will never be combed out. If I were to try we'd both be bald. Instead, we brush over the tangles and leave them lie. My psychologist brother-in-law urges his clients to work things through, not to allow old wounds to fester. But sometimes it is best to leave the infected spot alone. If it's poked and squeezed it can spread and become worse. When left to itself the pus is assimilated back into the body. There is more than one way for the body to heal.

The camel slips around out of sight when I come in the room. I help Jeanne get to the bathroom and to her chair for a breathing treatment. I bring a light meal and her medicines. She naps morning and evening, like my babies did, years ago. When newborn Laurie stared out toward the bright window beyond the crib, Jeanne said that the baby watched angels.

Many times now Jeanne sits gazing out her bedroom window. When I leave the room, the camel comes right up to the window and looks in. Neither of them looks away.

The final words of the Cinderella fairy tale form a concluding snapshot. The glass slipper fits and the narration sprints to the happily ever after like a child dashing to get in the family photo. Prince and princess pose smiling on the castle steps with the queen mother-in-law standing unobtrusively in the background. All is well forevermore in the castle.

Not so with the Arabian version. After the anklet fits, the jealous sisters take possession of the alabaster pot and become mistresses of the genie. At their bidding the genie conjures enchanted hairpins. The sisters dress the bride's hair for the wedding, and when the last lovely hairpin is placed in her curls, she is transformed to a dove. Frightened, she flies out the castle window.

The prince is heartbroken at the mysterious loss of his bride. As he mourns, a bird at his window sings sweetly to comfort him. This bird seems so tame that he reaches out his finger to see if she will light on it. Holding the bird he sees the hairpins tangled in her feathers and he begins to remove them. When the last hairpin falls from her feathers she again becomes the youngest sister, his bride. So the story finally arrives at its happy ending.

Where is the happily ever after in a pimply cyst? The ugly things cling and tangle. Even when I root them out, they reappear. What's the use?

I was the little girl in a hurry. I learned to read, to write quick and messy cursive, to recite my times tables faster than anyone else in third grade. Behind closed doors the girl I was wrote versions of her own happily ever after in a sky blue diary. Always in the future. Always just beyond the next hurdle. College, a boyfriend, Syria, a fiancé, marriage, a baby, buy a house with Grandma, a stable life . . . always I am longing for the happy ending.

I keep coming up short.

Happiness in this life comes braided with hardship. This primeval ache for things to be made right, for harmony between us—this is not a childish thing to be left behind. Longing forms the braid's third strand.

My daughter takes a shower every night. When she gets out, her hair smells of jasmine, just like a night breeze in the Middle East. I draw her close and I caress the damp tangles.

CPSIA information can be obtained at www.ICGtesting.com
227370LV00001B/133/P